PRICE THEORY AND PRICE POLICY

D1487997

Price Theory
and
Price Policy

M. A. G. van Meerhaeghe

LONGMANS

LONGMANS, GREEN AND CO LTD
London and Harlow

*Associated companies, representatives and agents
throughout the world*

© Longmans, Green & Co Ltd, 1969
First published 1969
SBN 582 50005 2

*Printed in Great Britain by
Butler & Tanner Ltd, Frome and London*

Contents

Contents

Contents

Preface

When a number of my friends suggested that I might publish a collection of some of my articles on price theory and price policy, I was pleased—*vanitas vanitatum*—to do as they proposed. None the less, I am fully aware of the drawbacks of such a collection: cohesion between the various contributions will inevitably leave much to be desired, and uniformity of treatment will generally be lacking too. The writers usually do not have the time to revise their material completely or (and this is more essential, as a rule) to expand it adequately. This second point applies in my particular case at any rate. However, each of the contributions presented here has been amended and brought up to date, mainly in order to prevent over-lapping and obtain the minimum of cohesion.

The first chapter deals with 'Market structure, market behaviour and market performance': a survey of these concepts and their interrelation appears to be a good introduction to the subsequent chapters. Some of it has been taken from Part 1 of my book *Marktvormen, marktgedrag en marktresultaten in België* (Ghent 1963).

Chapters 2 and 3 are devoted to price theory and price policy respectively. Chapter 2 reproduces a lecture, hitherto unpublished, delivered to the members of the *Institut des Reviseurs d'Entreprises* in Brussels on 9 March 1968. The original text of Chapter 3 appeared in the July 1967 issue of the French journal *Revue Economique*.

In Chapters 4 and 5 two instruments of price policy are studied in greater detail: competition policy, because there is still a great deal of confusion about this subject; advance notification of price increases, because no study dealing solely with this matter has hitherto been published. The texts concerned appeared originally in the December 1967 issue of the Austrian review *Zeitschrift für Nationalökonomie* and the February 1968 issue of the Swiss journal *Kyklos*.

In view of the fact that the Belgian Prices Commission has features that are not to be found in any other country, Chapter 6—which may be considered a sequel to Chapter 5—reproduces a text on this body which was originally published in the German periodical *Weltwirtschaftliches Archiv* (1967, Band 99, Heft 2).

The collection may be divided into two parts. The first three chapters endeavour to provide as concise as possible a statement of the current state of economic science. Although they represent my personal standpoint, they add nothing to knowledge. They are designed chiefly for the student who has already made some headway in the subject and for the graduate who has not been able to keep up with the problems involved. The last three chapters cover less familiar ground and may be of interest not only to students but also to my fellow economists.

Needless to say, the views expressed in the present publication are not necessarily shared by the members of the Belgian Prices Commission, of which I have the honour to be Chairman.

I am grateful to the editors of the aforementioned journals for their permission to make use of material published in their pages.

My thanks are also due to Mr. John Cairns and Mr. Leonard Scott for their painstaking efforts in the translation of this book. Mr. Cairns translated Chapters 3, 5 and 6, Mr. Scott Chapters 1, 2 and 4.

Finally, I must thank my assistant, Mr. F. Dernicourt, for his help in assembling documentary material, compiling the indexes and correcting the proofs.

November 1968   M. A. G. VAN
MEERHAEGHE

1 Market structure, market conduct and market performance

This is an inquiry into the interrelation of market structure, conduct and performance. After enlarging on these three concepts as such, we shall endeavour chiefly to determine the influence of structure and conduct on performance. As we shall see directly, the latter is closely bound up with the level of prices.

A. DEFINITIONS[1]

Before defining market organization and structure, market conduct and market performance, we remind our readers that *market* is here understood in its general sense of a group of buyers (demand) and sellers (supply) in contact with one another.

1. Market organization and structure

The circumstances in which a product changes hands can be subdivided into two groups—market organization and market structure. Market organization relates to the technical means by which buyers and sellers can come into contact (e.g. exchanges, shops, travelling salesmen), the route followed by goods and services between producer and consumer (the distribution system) and the government regulations affecting transactions. Market structure relates to the features of the market that determine the nature of the relations between buyers and sellers, particularly power relationships.

1 See also M. A. G. van Meerhaeghe, *Handboek van de economie* (5th edn, Leiden 1966), pp. 195–203.

These two types of circumstances have an influence on each other: just as a given organization will facilitate or put obstacles in the way of a specific structure, so will a given structure entail a specific organization.

2. Market conduct

Market conduct or policy comprises the means employed by economic transactors (particularly suppliers) to achieve their aims. This can be subdivided into market strategy and market tactics—action of a general and of a more limited scope respectively.[2]

Restrictive agreements are best studied from the angle of market conduct (not market structure). Although agreements of this kind affect the powers of the various transactors, the actual number of transactors is not changed (as it is in the case of a trust or a selling agreement).

Again, there is a close link between market organization and structure and market policy: the former have an impact on policy options, and market policy is often used in an attempt to determine both the organization and the structure of the market.

3. Market performance

Market performance refers to the way in which the market fulfils its function and, for instance, contributes to the efficient operation and growth of the economy, full employment and an equitable distribution of income. More particularly, market performance is judged by prices because the objectives just named can hardly be attained if prices are not stable (see Chapter 3). Account must also be taken, however, of other factors such as the quality of the goods sold. In other words, we must examine whether prices are not too far removed from a normal level.

4. The perfect market

A perfect market is a market where there is only one price for any given product at any given time.[3] For this to be possible, any two

2 Many authors equate market conduct with market strategy, but we see no reason why normal usage should be abandoned.
3 Cf. W. S. Jevons' *Law of indifference* in his *The theory of political economy* (London 1871), p. 91; see also H. von Stackelberg, *Grundlagen der theoretischen Volkswirtschaftslehre* (Berne 1948), p. 219.

examples of the same product must be utterly identical (so that they can be exchanged at will) and buyers and sellers must have perfect knowledge of market conditions (market 'transparency'). There must be no scope for the expression of personal preference. As L. Baudin neatly puts it, it takes no more than a sales girl's smile to disrupt competition.[4]

Producers of a given article or type of good differentiate their products from those of their competitors by details of, for instance, taste, smell, colour, durability, packaging and brand name.[5] Advertising is an important factor here. Differentiation is found not only in virtually all consumer goods but also in many capital goods; however, the output of agriculture is still mostly homogeneous.

A good can be defined narrowly or broadly. Increasing product differentiation has ensured that the broader concept is the more widely accepted. For instance, a good does not comprise one particular brand of (say) cigarettes alone but all the other brands denoting substitute products as well. In other words, varieties with the same basic features but showing incidental differences constitute a market as long as they satisfy identical needs; the firms producing them constitute a single industry.

On a perfect ('transparent') market buyers and sellers have knowledge of all the elements of the market: buyers know the prices at which suppliers are willing to sell, and sellers know the prices buyers are prepared to pay. 'Transparency' of the market does not mean that participants know and can foresee everything but that they are sufficiently informed to take advantage of any difference in price[6]— and are ready to do so. Contacts between buyers and sellers are not obstructed. Where 'transparency' of the market is lacking, price disparities can be maintained.

This is connected with the homogeneity of goods: where there are many differentiated products, it is difficult to assess market

---

4 L. Baudin, *La monnaie et la formation des prix* (3rd edn, Paris 1947), p. 203, already cited in the second edition of our *Handboek van de economie* (1958).

5 Different prices can also be charged for homogeneous products—if the conditions of sale are different, for instance atmosphere, heating, personal relations. This is not what is meant by product differentiation.

6 Sometimes—wrongly—an extraordinarily rapid response is required (E. Gutenberg, *Grundlagen der Betriebswirtschaftslehre, Teil II: Der Absatz*, 4th edn, Berlin 1962, p. 166). This is not very convincing: consumer habits are not susceptible of immediate change. Changes in production also take time, especially when new production factors have to be introduced. Distance cuts down labour mobility. Delivery dates may delay the availability of raw materials and auxiliary goods. However, these factors need not detract from the unity of price at a given time or the perfection of the market.

conditions. Perfect knowledge of the market is in any case unlikely if we take spatial considerations into account: distance can be an impediment.

B. MARKET STRUCTURE

Various criteria can be employed to indicate the nature of the relationship between buyers and sellers, particularly the degree of perfection of the market and freedom of entry to the market, together with the number and relative importance of buyers and sellers.

1. Perfect and pure competition

There is perfect competition when the following conditions prevail:

a. perfection of the market[7]
b. no barriers to the entry of new firms
c. a large number of buyers and sellers, so that no one can influence total supply or total demand substantially by changing his own demand or supply; in other words, each buyer or seller regards the market price as independent of his personal decisions
d. complete mobility of the factors of production.

Where only the first three of these conditions prevail (without market 'transparency') there is pure competition. Even this type of competition existed only to a limited extent in the mid-nineteenth century; at the moment imperfect competition prevails everywhere.

2. Imperfect competition

a. As we have noted, there are no perfect markets. Product differentiation gives every producer a monopoly in his own products, though this situation is seriously challenged by the many possibilities of substitution. Here we speak of monopolistic or heterogeneous or differentiated competition (oligopoly or duopoly where there are a small number of sellers or only two: see below). Interindustry competition is also strong in some cases (e.g. between metal and plastic products).
b. Established firms or the financing institutions controlling them

---

7 A perfect market does not imply perfect competition: even in a monopoly or oligopoly situation there may be only one price on a given market.

do their utmost to exclude new firms. As a matter of fact, increasingly large sums are needed to set up a firm. And then there is no certainty that a new firm will immediately be able to produce under optimum circumstances since this requires a minimum output. Moreover, additional factors of production (e.g. skilled workers) are not always available. And account must be taken of buyers' preference for existing brands.

J. S. Bain distinguishes between 'easy entry', 'ineffectively impeded entry', 'effectively impeded entry' and 'blockaded entry'.[8]

As product differentiation is becoming more and more widespread, easy entry only makes sense if the boundaries of the market are drawn broadly so as to include substitute products as well. This concept of the market is relatively vague. The same holds good for the concept of industry. Following N. Kaldor,[9] R. Triffin has therefore worked out a different method of classifying markets,[10] making use of cross elasticities. The drawback, however, is that cross elasticities cannot in fact be calculated.

c. Many producers go out of business as a result of competition itself, which gives rise to such things as trusts and restrictive agreements between competitors. Depending on the number of sellers, we have monopoly (one seller), duopoly (two), oligopoly (few) and polypoly (many); on the buyers' side we have mono-, duo-, oligo- and polypsony. Various combinations are therefore possible (a simple example being given in the table overleaf).[11]

The indistinct boundary between 'many' and 'few' is determined by considering what influence a single seller (or buyer) has on other sellers (or buyers). If his influence is perceptible, we have 'few' sellers (or buyers), otherwise 'many'.

The relative importance of buyers and sellers (or their market share) is also a significant factor. Where there is a single big seller and few or many small sellers, we have a partial monopoly;[12]

8 J. S. Bain, *Barriers to new competition. Their character and consequences in manufacturing industries* (Cambridge, Mass., 1956), pp. 21–2.

9 N. Kaldor, 'Mrs Robinson's "Economics of imperfect competition"', *Economica*, Aug 1934; N. Kaldor, 'Market imperfection and excess capacity', *Economica*, Feb 1935.

10 R. Triffin, *Monopolistic competition and general equilibrium theory* (Cambridge, Mass., 1940), pp. 117–23, 143. Triffin was inspired by Chamberlin's way of distinguishing the large from the small group; see E. H. Chamberlin, *The theory of monopolistic competition. A re-orientation of the theory of value* (7th edn, Cambridge, Mass., 1958), p. 83.

11 More complicated subdivisions can be found in, e.g., F. J. de Jong, *Het systeem van de marktvormen* (Leiden 1951), p. 155, and K. Brandt, *Preistheorie* (Ludwigshafen 1960), p. 11.

12 Where there are two (or few) big and many small sellers, we have partial duopoly (or partial oligopoly).

where the oligopolists are of gradually declining size (with every firm having to take account of smaller competitors), we have proposed the term 'pyramid' oligopoly.[13]

The statistics available generally oblige us to analyse market structure on the basis of the number and relative importance of buyers and sellers.

Market structure

Supply Demand	One seller	Few sellers	Many sellers
One buyer	bilateral monopoly	limited monopsony	monopsony
Few buyers	limited monopoly	bilateral oligopoly	oligopsony
Many buyers	monopoly	oligopoly	bilateral polypoly

3. Oligopoly

Oligopoly is the most frequently occurring market structure. It is difficult to give precise details on the point because the concept is not clear-cut. An arbitrary boundary always has to be drawn.

About a third of American industries are oligopolies in which the largest eight firms make at least 50 per cent of shipments and the largest twenty firms at least 75 per cent. Another third are weaker oligopolies (with the eight leading firms making at least 33 per cent of shipments and the top twenty less than 75 per cent). In other industries with a low degree of concentration the biggest eight firms make less than 33 per cent of shipments.[14]

In Belgium, 77 per cent of the industries investigated by the present writer are partial monopolies, 'pyramid' oligopolies and oligopolies proper (true oligopolies with sellers of about the same size are very infrequent), 8·2 per cent are monopolies and 4·8 per cent atomistic; the remaining 10 per cent are marginal cases. Concentration is even higher if we take financial links into account (control of holding

---

13 M. A. G. van Meerhaeghe, *Marktvormen, marktgedrag en marktresultaten in België* (Ghent 1963) p. 12.

14 *Concentration ratios in manufacturing industry 1963. Part I* (Bureau of the Census, Washington 1966).

companies): this is the situation in coalmining, the cement industry and the manufacture of paper and paperboard.[15]

C. MARKET CONDUCT

In the study of how to classify market behaviour, pioneering work was done by K. Sting[16] and R. Frisch.[17] E. Schneider improved Frisch's system,[18] and A. E. Ott carried work on the classification of conduct a step further.[19]

A distinction is usually made between price or quantity adjustments (in conditions of pure competition only quantities can be adjusted), interdependent price or quantity adjustments (account being taken of the reactions of other sellers) and policy regarding conflict and negotiation.

1. Competition

Where there is pure competition, the firm really cannot take any independent action. Price is determined by the market, and there is little point in advertising (since there is no product differentiation). Nor has the monopolist any freedom of choice—at least not if he wants to maximize his profit, though he is not obliged to pursue this objective. In other situations, particularly oligopoly, there is a greater range of options (see below). The instruments of market conduct (e.g. price and advertising) which are lacking in pure competition can now be used.

Competition as a type of market structure, or pure competition, should therefore be carefully distinguished from competition as a type of market conduct, or active competition. The latter can only exist where pure competition is absent.

15 These are 1959–60 figures. See M. A. G. van Meerhaeghe, *op. cit. supra* note 1. 13, p. 147. A summary of the major findings of this survey can be found in M. A. G. van Meerhaeghe, 'Die Marktformen, das Marktverhalten und die Marktergebnisse in Belgien', *Zeitschrift für die gesamte Staatswissenschaft,* Jan 1965.

16 K. Sting, 'Die polypolitische Preisbildung. Ein Kapitel der Preistheorie', *Jahrbücher für National-ökonomie und Statistik,* May 1931.

17 R. Frisch, 'Monopoly–polypoly. The concept of force in the economy', *International Economic Papers,* no. 1 (London 1951), (reprint of 'Monopole, polypole. La notion de force dans l'économie', *Nationaløkonomisk Tidsskrift,* Apr 1933).

18 E. Schneider, *Einführung in die Wirtschaftstheorie, II. Teil: Wirtschaftspläne und wirtschaftliches Gleichgewicht in der Verkehrswirtschaft* (10th edn, Tübingen 1965).

19 A. E. Ott, *Marktform und Verhaltensweise* (Stuttgart 1959), pp. 99–102.

Active competition, which implies rivalry and conflict, can take two forms:

a. effective, healthy or performance competition
b. non-performance competition.

The latter can take on various forms, including unfair competition (e.g. copying a trade mark), disorderly competition (when prices are manifestly too low owing to inadequate information on one's costs) and margin competition (competition in dealers' margins).

2. Oligopoly

Since cooperation in one field or another is the general rule in oligopolies, the study of uncoordinated oligopoly is of less importance.

Firms in a given industry usually meet to discuss matters of common interest. One of the effects of these meetings is to tone down competition: firms usually have fewer scruples about taking customers away from strangers than from colleagues.[20] Trade associations often establish good conduct codes themselves; for instance, they lay down rules for the calculation of prices. Sometimes members notify their intention of increasing prices, and a certain period is allowed to lapse before the new prices take effect.

One of the oligopolists will often take the initiative in market policy. His lead will then be followed by the others. This leading role may be assumed by different firms in succession. As a rule, only one or two of the leading oligopolist's products are affected—not his whole output. Price leadership is a phenomenon in which there are many barriers to entry, close substitute products, an elasticity of demand that is not much greater than unity, and almost identical cost curves.[21] The price leader may act as a sort of barometer—when his price is regarded by the other sellers as a reliable reflection of market conditions ('barometric' price leadership as opposed to 'dominant' price leadership). He cannot oblige the others to follow: the convention generally depends on tacit agreement.[22]

In the case of 'pyramid' oligopoly, small and medium-sized

20 A. R. Oxenfeldt, D. Miller, A. Shuchman and C. Winick, *Insights into pricing. From operation research and behavioral science* (Belmont, Cal., 1961), pp. 115–17.
21 J. W. Markham, 'The nature and significance of price leadership', *The American Economic Review*, Dec 1951, pp. 902–3.
22 R. F. Lanzillotti, 'Competitive price leadership: a critique of price leadership models', *The Review of Economics and Statistics*, Feb 1957, p. 59.

competitors follow changes in price only if they find it to their advantage.[23] They are inclined to undersell in order to compensate for the consumer's lack of familiarity with their brands (low brand acceptance) and their limited product variation (see Chapter 2, C, 2). They are often prompted to take this course because they are short of liquid assets. Because their share of the market is so small, they expect no reaction from the big firms.

Where all the sellers in a given industry conclude an agreement and abide by it, we have 'complete collusion'.[24] This sort of cartel can be formed more easily if all the members are about equally powerful and if the agreement is in the interests of them all[25]—which means that the different firms' costs must be virtually the same.

In price-fixing agreements, all the parties—or a delegated number of them—agree to charge a single price. Compliance is sometimes enforced by fines or reprisals. In many cases, sales are also regulated (each firm being assigned a quota of the industry's total sales or output), and the market is generally shared out as well.[26] A 'profit pool' may be set up in order to obviate any jealousy. Joint sales can only work if the products concerned are fairly homogeneous.

These agreements are often infringed. For instance, some suppliers quietly set their prices lower. And where the rules are vague, those participating also have a certain amount of elbow room. Where complete collusion is impaired in this way, the advantages of monopoly do not altogether materialize.[27]

Oligopolists usually prefer to keep some degree of freedom so as to increase and exploit their negotiating powers. For instance, they may refuse to cut down on product differentiation or advertising, to pool their brands, to locate production units so as to keep freight costs low, or to use installations jointly. Reductions in price are often not carried out, even though they would increase the joint profit, and in periods of expansion excessive increases are made.

3. Administered prices

Administered prices are found both in oligopolies and in monopolies. They are determined not by the interplay of supply and

23 Cf. J. W. Markham, *supra* note 1.21, p. 901.
24 Cf. J. S. Bain, *Industrial organization* (2nd edn, New York 1968), p. 306.
25 *Ibid.*, pp. 323–4.
26 F. Machlup, *The political economy of monopoly* (Baltimore 1952), p. 95.
27 F. Machlup, *The economics of sellers' competition* (Baltimore 1952), p. 476.

demand but by corporate or government decision.[28] Once fixed, administered prices are not changed unless there are more or less definitive changes in costs or shifts in demand; they are, in fact, rather rigid.[29]

D. MARKET STRUCTURE AND MARKET CONDUCT

The importance of market structure for price determination is influenced by the extent to which a given policy can be identified with each type. Older writers, who could see no further than pure competition and monopoly, took this for granted. Doubts were not raised until oligopoly and bilateral monopoly began to be studied.

K. Sting considers that a given policy will probably but not necessarily be pursued in a given type of market.[30] According to R. Frisch, pure competition goes together with quantity adjustment and partial monopoly with autonomous action. It is only in the intermediate types of structure, particularly bilateral monopoly and oligopoly, that there is a range of possible policies.[31]

For E. Schneider, there is for the most part no connection between market structure and market conduct.[32] It is not the number of sellers or their relative size that is important but each seller's view of his own position. For instance, if one of a group of ten sellers considers himself a monopolist and behaves accordingly, then he *is* a monopolist, according to Schneider. On the other hand, if the sole producer of a good does not consider himself a monopolist, because substitute products are available, he must be regarded as an oligopolist or a polypolist. Schneider therefore concludes that the only thing that is relevant as regards how the economic process unfolds is the conduct of buyers and sellers; their structural relations are basically unimportant.[33]

28 M. A. G. van Meerhaeghe, *op. cit. supra* note 1.1, p. 229. For other definitions of administered prices, see J. F. Weston, 'Statement' in *Employment, growth and price levels. Hearings 86th Congress* (Washington 1959), p. 2295. Cf. J. M. Keynes, *The general theory of employment, interest and money* (London 1936), p. 268.

29 For a review of the literature, see J. Cédras, 'Prix administrés: faits et théories', *Revue Economique*, Jul 1962. See also Chapter 3, C, 2c.

30 K. Sting, *supra* note 1.16, pp. 763–4.

31 R. Frisch, *supra* note 1.17, pp. 31–2.

32 He does assume, however, that quantities are always adjusted in conditions of atomistic, homogeneous competition.

33 E. Schneider, *op. cit. supra* note 1.18, p. 72. See also W. Eucken, *Die Grundlagen der National-ökonomie* (7th edn, Berlin 1959), pp. 218–19.

A. E. Ott gives more attention to the degree of perfection of the market in his study of the link between market conduct and market structure.[34] Following W. A. Jöhr,[35] he characterizes the influence of the number and relative size of buyers and sellers as 'independence', 'dependence' and 'interdependence'. Typical examples of the first and last are monopoly and oligopoly, respectively. Polypoly, on the other hand, is a binary phenomenon: each individual seller is independent of any other seller, but all the competitors are jointly dependent on each other.

The more imperfect a market (as a result of product differentiation, lack of knowledge of the market, etc.), the greater the degree of independence. An oligopoly can disintegrate into a series of monopoly positions. In oligopoly on a perfect market the seller must take account of his competitors' reactions. He can decide what his optimum policy should be only when he knows how his rivals will behave: he is obliged to form some idea of what they will do. The same holds good for bilateral monopoly.

Except for polypoly, market structures seem to have no definite link with market conduct. We can only say definitely that some type of conduct (we do not know which) goes together with a certain market structure. More specifically, this is because oligopoly is a blanket term covering situations that are often extremely divergent. So the distinction between those writers who do find a fixed relationship between structure and conduct and those who do not is not really so great. What is probable is that buyers and sellers will take objective market conditions into account in the long run.

Although J. S. Bain also considers that it is difficult to establish systematic associations between structure and conduct, he does note a few general tendencies in industry in the United States.[36]

a. The higher the degree of concentration, the more action is interdependent without evident collusion. Instances of collusive arrangements are more frequent in industries of moderate concentration than in highly concentrated industries (mutually advantageous interdependent conduct without collusion is less probable than in the case of high concentration).

34 A. E. Ott, *op. cit. supra* note 1.19, pp. 114 *et seq.*
35 W. A. Jöhr, 'Regulation of competition', in *Monopoly and competition and their regulation* (ed. E. H. Chamberlin, London 1954), p. 342.
36 J. S. Bain, *op. cit. supra* note 1.24, pp. 330–1.

b. Where there is evident collusion, it is less perfect where concentration is low than where it is high.

c. A high degree of product differentiation generally leads to simple interdependence without collusion (not necessarily to identical prices).

d. The height of barriers to entry seems to have no influence on coordination between sellers.

Bain also lists a number of theoretically likely types of conduct in the case of non-independent pricing.[37] For instance, high concentration and high barriers to entry will be more conducive to joint profit maximization than low concentration and ease of entry. If this is so, high concentration should also lead to higher prices and perhaps greater restriction of output.

E. MARKET PERFORMANCE

Various criteria may be employed to judge whether prices are 'normal'—for instance, the level of profits and selling costs, the flexibility of prices, and plant size.

1. Profits

High profits are not objectionable in themselves: they may be needed to finance new investment or more research. But if they become permanent and are mainly used to pay out dividends, prices could be reduced instead.

2. Distribution and selling costs

It is not always easy to distinguish between expenditure incurred in promoting sales and the cost of distribution, particularly as both have an impact on sales.

High promotional costs make it difficult to cut prices. The bigger the sums involved, the more unlikely it is that prices will be cut. Market entry is also hindered in industries where selling costs are high (see Chapter 2, C, 3).

3. Plant size

A study needs to be made of whether plants produce in optimum circumstances. Many plants are too small, but big ones do not *ipso*

37 J. S. Bain, *op. cit. supra* note 1.24, pp. 331–2.

facto produce more cheaply than smaller ones. Capacity must be put to work almost to the limit; a small volume of surplus capacity is justifiable with a view to periods of more intensive demand. Generalization on this point is difficult.

Optimum plant size differs from one industry to the next. Studies carried out in twenty American industries showed that the optimum scale of a plant was between 10 and 20 per cent of the market in six industries (fountain pens, tractors, copper, gypsum products, typewriters and automobiles), 5 or 6 per cent in five industries (cigarettes, soap, rayon fibre, farm machinery and steel), less than 5 per cent in the others (and even below 2 per cent in flour milling, liquor distilling and fresh meat packing). Inefficient firms accounted for between 10 and 30 per cent of the market, depending on the industry.[38]

4. Price flexibility

Various opinions are held on price flexibility.[39] They can be subdivided into two main groups, depending on whether a relative or an absolute approach is adopted.

In the relative approach, changes in price are compared with changes in other factors. Price flexibility as generally understood refers to the change in price relative to a change in quantity;[40] this is the reciprocal of elasticity of demand. However, the concept is also used in a more general sense—referring to the extent to which prices react to changes in certain factors, or simply referring to the extent of their variability.

Most writers relate changes in price to changes in elements of cost. This is logical, since lasting cost reductions should normally be reflected in price.

J. T. Dunlop[41] relates the extent of the variation of marginal costs to that of prices, employing A. P. Lerner's measure of monopoly (the difference between price and marginal cost, divided by price).[42] A kindred view is that of R. Ruggles: perfect price flexibility is the

---

38 *Ibid.*, pp. 191, 379.
39 Discussed by R. Ruggles, 'The nature of price flexibility and the determinants of relative price changes in the economy', in *Business concentration and price policy* (Princeton 1955), pp. 450–60.
40 See, e.g., F. C. Mills, *Price-quantity interactions in business cycles* (New York 1946), p. 16.
41 J. T. Dunlop, 'Price flexibility and the "degree of monopoly"', *The Quarterly Journal of Economics*, Aug 1939, pp. 522–33.
42 A. P. Lerner, *The economics of control. Principles of welfare economics* (New York 1944), p. 361.

situation where price changes by the same percentage as marginal cost; if it changes less, the price is inflexible; if it changes more, it is excessively flexible; if it moves in the opposite direction, it is inversely flexible.[43]

As marginal costs, however, are difficult to determine, the utility of these methods is slight. Moreover, they take no account of changes in demand.

For this reason, many writers study absolute changes in price. G. C. Means, for instance, has investigated the frequency of price changes in the United States between 1926 and 1933.[44] A classification of products according to degree of variability in price gives two price categories—flexible and inflexible. According to G. C. Means, the first are determined by the market, the second by corporate managements. He also notes that during the depression the greater the variability, the more significant the price decrease. Nevertheless, the borderline between flexible and inflexible prices is often difficult to find.

To investigate the flexibility of wholesale and retail prices in Belgium, the present writer has calculated variability indices for the years 1950–61 and the extent of price changes.[45]

Although the classification into flexible and inflexible prices is somewhat arbitrary, more than half of wholesale prices do show predominantly inflexible characteristics; and inflexibility is greater in respect of reductions in price than in respect of increases. A smaller proportion (25 per cent) are flexible—with the opposite tendency, though not as marked—and finally there is a mixed group.

The increases in inflexible prices are generally bigger than the reductions; on the other hand, flexible prices tend to rise or fall by much the same percentage.

The retail prices investigated were found to change quite appreciably: more than 60 per cent of them are flexible and less than 10 per cent inflexible. Inflexibility in respect of reductions, however, is even more pronounced than in the case of wholesale prices. Average percentage changes are smaller.

43 R. Ruggles, *supra* note 1.39, p. 463.
44 G. C. Means, 'The problem of price inflexibility', in *Price practices and price policies* (ed. J. Backman, New York 1953), pp. 45–9.
45 M. A. G. van Meerhaeghe, *op. cit. supra* note 1.13, Chapter 15.

F. EFFECTS OF STRUCTURE AND CONDUCT ON PERFORMANCE

In the same way as we have studied the relation between market structure and conduct, we will now go on to examine whether there is any definite association between market structure and/or conduct and market performance.

1. Market structure

While it is true that monopolies and oligopolies can have many drawbacks (such as excessively high prices, profits and advertising costs, curbs on technical advance and barriers to entry), they often produce the corresponding advantages (lower prices, higher expenditure on research—which promotes industrial innovation).

Once again, it is not easy to make general pronouncements. The most divergent types of structure may yield satisfactory performance. Furthermore, few studies have been made of the links between structure and performance.

His researches into twenty American industries brought J. S. Bain to the conclusion that high concentration entails bigger profits,[46] especially where there are high barriers to entry as well. The relation of excess profits to product differentiation is even clearer, as are the links between product differentiation and the number of inefficient plants: the higher the one, the bigger the other. There seems to be no connection between the scale of inefficient plants and concentration or barriers to entry. Product differentiation and selling costs move in the same direction.[47]

The leading plants often prove bigger than is really required: in other words, concentration is unnecessarily high. This seems to be particularly the case with vertical integration.[48]

As regards the effect of concentration on price flexibility, W. L. Thorp and W. F. Crowder found no marked difference between highly concentrated and unconcentrated industries in the United States.[49] A. C. Neal considers that concentration is insufficient of

---

46 No such findings were made in Belgium. See M. A. G. van Meerhaeghe, *ibid.*, p. 299.

47 In this connection we would note L. G. Telser's comment: 'There is little empirical support for the proposition that the more advertising employed in industry, the less competitive it is likely to be, despite some plausible theorizing to the contrary', 'Advertising and competition', *The Journal of Political Economy*, Dec 1964, p. 558.

48 J. S. Bain, *op. cit. supra* note 1.24, pp. 380–1.

49 W. L. Thorp and W. F. Crowder, *The structure of industry* (Washington 1947), pp. 411–12.

itself to explain the differences in price changes during a depression.[50] R. S. Tucker and E. M. Doblin deny that there is any connection at all.[51]

The sample relied on in Belgium to investigate the connection between wholesale prices and concentration does not provide basis enough for unassailable conclusions. However, the monopolistic, partially monopolistic and oligopolistic industries do tend to lead to inflexible prices; this confirms the similar findings in our analysis of market conduct. The sparse material available on retail prices indicates no such link.[52]

Finally, the structure of demand has an impact on market performance. There are normally negotiations between the two parties to a bilateral monopoly. Here, negotiating power is of primary importance. Compared with monopoly, bilateral monopoly shows a level of prices coming closer to that of bilateral polypoly. This is also true of coordinated oligopsony (e.g. joint purchasing of raw materials) as opposed to monopoly.

'Pyramid' oligopsony, however, gives rise to individual purchases, and the monopolist makes use of these to practise price discrimination. Department stores, for instance, can buy goods more cheaply than non-integrated retail firms. In a sellers' market the advantages of a strong position of power are not always seen in cheaper purchase prices but in assured supplies.

Where a 'pyramid' oligopoly is accompanied by an oligopsony, the big sellers cannot impose conditions of sale to the same extent as a monopolist. For buyers have some choice of sources of supply, and substitute products are generally available too. On a market where supply is atomistic and demand concentrated, even lower prices than in a bilateral polypoly are possible.

2. Market conduct

Here again, it is difficult to establish links with market performance. Conduct that seems to be aimed at maximizing joint profits will

---

50 A. C. Neal, 'Industrial concentration and price inflexibility' (American Council on Public Affairs), quoted in *Relationship of prices to economic stability and growth. Hearings 85th Congress* (Washington 1959), pp. 632–5.

51 R. S. Tucker, 'Concentration and competition', *The Journal of Marketing*, Apr 1940, quoted in *Relationship of prices to economic stability and growth, op. cit. supra* note 1.50, pp. 635–6; E. M. Doblin, 'Some aspects of price inflexibility', *The Review of Economic Statistics*, Nov 1940, pp. 185–6.

52 M. A. G. van Meerhaeghe, *op. cit. supra* note 1.13, Chapter 15.

also be inspired by other considerations in fact, such as fear of potential competition, mistrust of competitors, and the possibility that less efficient plants will be better equipped as a result of higher profits (see Chapter 2, B).

Administered prices are becoming more and more frequent. Product differentiation is becoming *the* means of competition. Some degree of real price competition is found among department stores, but not as much as there might be in view of their organization.

We find more evidence in respect of structure and performance where there is aggressive conduct. A price war (a very rare occurrence) sometimes sends small competitors out of business and excludes new market entrants. The same result can be achieved by a firm gaining control of transport systems. In such cases market structure (higher concentration or higher barriers to entry) and market performance (prices) are directly influenced by market conduct.

3. Conclusion

It is no wonder that growing interest is being shown in the study of the interaction of market structure, conduct and performance. The regulation of market performance involves direct government intervention; this is not always politically possible and may indeed have its drawbacks. But if there were a connection between specific market structures and performance, the government could act on performance through these structures. It could also try to influence market conduct if there were a similar correlation between structure and conduct.

As we have shown, however, it is difficult to formulate generally valid conclusions. This is partly because too few investigations have been made and because conditions vary from industry to industry. Any given structure can have good or bad effects, depending on circumstances. There is consequently no justification for giving preference to a specific market structure, as do some countries and international organizations.

2 Price theory and reality

Although criticism of the current or neoclassical theory of price, which is based on marginalist principles, is nothing new, little or no attention is paid to it in most economics textbooks.

Here we shall sum up the major objections to marginalism in price theory, going on to discuss managerial objectives and the instruments of marketing policy. Lastly, we state the conclusions that we think can be drawn from the present state of affairs.

A. CRITICISM OF MARGINALISM

According to marginal price theory, profit maximization is the basic principle by which the producer is guided in determining his prices. In order to maximize his profits (or minimize his losses), he attempts to equate marginal cost[1] to marginal revenue. As long as marginal revenue exceeds marginal cost, it is to his advantage to increase output. Since marginal cost is not affected by the level of fixed costs, this does not tell us whether the firm's average total costs in respect of the output in question are covered. We must therefore investigate whether they are or not.

The information we have on producers' behaviour on this point[2]

---

1 Not to be confused with differential or incremental cost. Marginal cost is the additional cost that a producer incurs by making *one* additional unit of output.

2 Disregarding special cases (such as the experiments of *Electricité de France*) in which 'sale at marginal cost does not necessarily produce budgetary equilibrium': M. Boiteux, 'Electric energy: facts, problems and prospects', in *Marginal cost pricing in practice* (ed. J. R. Nelson, Englewood Cliffs 1964), p. 25.

shows, however, that firms employ other methods of pricing and in most cases do not even know the meaning of marginal cost and revenue. As K. E. Boulding puts it, 'Most people who actually set prices seem to get along very well without (the rather forbidding mass of literature known as price theory)'.[3]

The general use of full-cost pricing (absorption costing)—fully allocated cost plus a fixed or variable profit margin—has been illustrated by R. L. Hall, C. J. Hitch,[4] W. J. Eiteman,[5] P. J. D. Wiles[6] and B. Fog,[7] among others.

Direct costing[8]—which came into prominence in the 1950s—does give some insight into cost calculation but provides little assistance in the determination of cost price and selling price.[9] Firms whose selling prices secure large profits but are not so much determined by cost prices will turn more quickly to direct costing—which is sometimes inaccurately called marginal costing.[10]

According to P. W. S. Andrews,[11] firms employ a 'normal' price. This is distinguished from the full-cost price in that it takes potential competition more into account, thus restricting the opportunity for immediate profits. Potential competition can come either from new firms or from existing firms (if they convert their production facilities).[12]

One of the objections to marginalism in fact is that it attaches no importance to long-term considerations. On the contrary, it assumes that changes in marginal cost and revenue are immediately reflected in changes in price. The continuous price fluctuations that result,

3 K. E. Boulding, 'The uses of price theory', in *Models of markets* (ed. A. R. Oxenfeldt, New York 1963), p. 146.
4 R. L. Hall and C. J. Hitch, 'Price theory and business behaviour', *Oxford Economic Papers*,
5 May 1939, reprinted in *Oxford Studies in the price mechanism* (eds. T. Wilson and P. W. S. Andrews, Oxford 1951).
6 W. J. Eiteman, *Price determination. Business practice versus economic theory* (Ann Arbor 1949). P. J. D. Wiles, *Price, cost and output* (Oxford 1956).
7 B. Fog, *Industrial pricing policies. An analysis of pricing policies of Danish manufacturers* (Amsterdam 1960).
8 Direct costs (which can be identified relatively easily with a specific unit of output) may be either fixed (the cost of a machine used to make a specific product) or variable (the cost of raw materials). Other costs are classified as indirect.
9 H. J. van der Schroeff, *Kosten en kostprijs* (5th edn, Amsterdam 1963), p. 486. See also W. Kilger, *Flexible Plankostenrechnung. Theorie und Praxis der Grenzplankostenrechnung und Deckungsbeitragsrechnung* (3rd edn, Cologne 1967).
10 See, e.g., F. C. Lawrence and E. N. Humphreys, *Marginal costing* (London 1947) ; J. P. de Bodt, *Critique économique du prix de revient industriel. Avec illustration concrète de l'utilisation de la méthode de la comptabilité marginale* (2nd edn, Louvain 1966).
11 P. W. S. Andrews, 'A reconsideration of the theory of the individual business', *Oxford Economic Papers*, Jan 1949, p. 81.
12 P. W. S. Andrews, *Manufacturing business* (London 1959), p. 176.

however, encourage speculation. Both dealers and consumers prefer price stability, which also makes it easier for firms to plan ahead. In other words, it is often better to let a short-term advantage go in order to safeguard long-term interests (by keeping potential competition in check).

Administered prices meet these requirements. Nearly all prices are now administered prices. Even producers of raw materials realize that they have an interest in keeping their prices stable—partly in order to exclude substitute products. This explains the efforts of the major copper, aluminium and zinc producers to set prices independently of fluctuations on the London Metal Exchange.[13] And in Belgium we find that the retail price of meat is held relatively stable despite fluctuations in the price of livestock.

Another objection to the marginalist principle is that it is impracticable: marginal cost and marginal revenue are generally impossible to calculate.

On the whole, the innumerable attempts to establish demand curves empirically have not met with success.[14] And the producer's view of demand is what counts in pricing by the marginal method. We should also remember that the consumer does not behave as rationally as is generally accepted: he normally buys under the influence of habit, fashion or advertising.

Marginal costs are particularly difficult to calculate in multi-product firms. Here it should be noted that neoclassical price theory pays no attention to the cost of sales promotion or distribution. The neoclassicists reason as though the producer and consumer were in direct touch with each other, which is not usually the case.

Lastly, the marginal method can be objected to on the grounds that it establishes the cheapest level of output. In reality the businessman sets his price; and only then does he consider what quantity he will be able to sell.

The supporters of marginalism do not take this lying down. As regards the criticism just mentioned, they maintain that the businessman does bear in mind expected sales when setting his price, so that output is taken into consideration indirectly.

The marginalists also believe that firms unconsciously follow the marginalist principle in constantly adapting gross profit margins to

13 A. Shonfield, *Modern capitalism. The changing balance of public and private power* (London 1965), pp. 364–5.
14 Cf. M. Friedman, *Price theory. A provisional text* (London 1962), pp. 33–4.

circumstances when applying full-cost and normal-cost pricing. If marginal costs remain constant—an assumption that is made increasingly often—the full-cost method corresponds to the marginal method (marginal costs and average variable costs coincide).

Again and again the marginalists disregard the point that it is not the facts that must be made to fit the theory but vice versa. One of the functions of theory is to illustrate the real state of affairs: its purpose is not, as many think,[15] to study a world of abstractions.

F. Machlup, who with E. Schneider[16] is one of the warmest advocates of the marginalist theory of the firm, finds no difficulty in the marginalist tenet that the firm is 'a theoretical construct' that should not be confused with 'a real organization'.[17] This, in his view, is not important as long as it is the 'theory of competitive price and allocation'[18] that is being considered.

This 'competitive price' is found but rarely, however, and it is therefore understandable that marginal theory produces so little result in the other, more frequent, market structures. For oligopoly pricing in particular, marginalism provides no elucidation. It remains—in spite of the use of the most refined mathematical aids—a 'disturbing and recalcitrant problem',[19] 'the real blind spot in price theory'.[20]

'Marginal theory of the firm', to quote Machlup again, 'should not be understood to imply anything but subjective estimates, guesses and hunches'.[21] How these are arrived at and what they really consist of, however, is not explained.[22]

Our criticism of marginalism does not imply that we regard price determination through absorption costing as the ideal method: only where the profit margin is constantly adjusted to demand is enough consideration given to demand. Where the profit margin is fixed, this is not so.

15 See, e.g., J. G. Knol, *Facetten van de moderne prijstheorie* (Haarlem 1965), pp. 12, 49.
16 E. Schneider, 'Der Realismus der Marginalanalyse in der Preistheorie', *Weltwirtschaftliches Archiv*, 73/1 (1954), reprinted in E. Schneider, *Volkswirtschaft und Betriebswirtschaft* (Tübingen 1964).
17 F. Machlup, 'Theories of the firm: marginalist, behavioral, managerial', *The American Economic Review*, Mar 1967, p. 4.
18 *Ibid.*, p. 15.
19 E. H. Chamberlin, 'On the origin of "oligopoly", *The Economic Journal*, Jun 1957, p. 218.
20 D. C. Hague, 'The task of the contemporary theory of pricing', in *Price formation in various countries. Proceedings of a Conference held by the International Economic Association* (ed. D. C. Hague, New York 1967), p. 9.
21 F. Machlup, 'Marginal analysis and empirical research', *The American Economic Review*, Sep 1946, p. 522.
22 J. L. Bouma, *Ondernemingsdoel en winst* (Leiden 1966), p. 45.

The full-cost price is just one of the many factors a businessman has to take into account when fixing his selling price.[23] Buyers, after all, know little or nothing of the manufacturer's cost.

We are not claiming that marginalist or related concepts are totally disregarded in management policies (e.g. direct costing or market research), but we do maintain that the central problem—the equality of marginal cost and marginal revenue—is not taken into account.

So far, our main criticism has been directed towards the technique of analysis. The real drawbacks to the current theory of price, however, are the two major assumptions on which it rests; although it is mentioned incidentally that businessmen can have objectives other than profit maximization, it is assumed that profit maximization is the only important aim; it is also assumed that price is the businessman's chief policy instrument, even when it is admitted that he may sometimes have others to rely upon. We shall deal with these two assumptions in turn.

B. MANAGERIAL OBJECTIVES

It is only by observation of businessmen's behaviour that we can analyse how they reach their decisions. Many empirical studies have been made on this basis. They show that as a general rule a variety of aims are pursued. Attempts have been made to examine the consequences of this fact for the theory of the firm.[24]

The main objectives of big firms in the United States seem to be target return on investment, stability of price and margin, a target market share, meeting or forestalling competition.[25] In Denmark small firms appear to aim at profit maximization in the short run, while big business, though it does not neglect profit maximization, pays more attention to long-term considerations.[26]

23 We do not dwell on these factors. See, e.g., A. R. Oxenfeldt, *Industrial policy and market policies* (New York 1951); D. V. Harper, *Price policy and procedure* (New York 1966).
24 See, e.g., K. E. Boulding, 'Implications for general economics of some realistic theories of the firm', *The American Economic Review*, May 1952; R. M. Cyert and J. G. March, 'Organizational factors in the theory of oligopoly', *The Quarterly Journal of Economics*, Feb 1956; E. O. Edwards, 'An indifference approach to the theory of the firm', *The Southern Economic Journal*, Oct 1961; R. M. Cyert and J. G. March, *A behavioral theory of the firm* (Englewood Cliffs 1963); O. E. Williamson, *The economics of discretionary behavior: managerial objectives in a theory of the firm* (Englewood Cliffs 1964).
25 R. F. Lanzillotti, 'Pricing objectives in large companies', *The American Economic Review*, Dec 1958.
26 B. Fog, *op. cit. supra* note 2.7, pp. 30–1.

The policy of the smaller firms can sometimes be explained by a shortage of liquid assets.

R. M. Cyert and J. G. March[27] conclude that the main objectives of the firm are a production goal, an inventory goal, a sales goal and a profit goal. These are, of course, closely linked.

W. J. Baumol believes that the principal objective is maximization of sales, at least as long as total profits do not fall beneath a specified minimum,[28] and more particularly maximization of the rate of growth of sales.[29] Satisfactory rather than maximum profit is what is important.[30]

Maximizing sales is a matter of prestige: a firm wants to keep if not increase its share of the market. At the same time, managers hope to demonstrate their professional skill, which—particularly in the more and more frequent cases where managers have little or no share in the firm's capital—may lead to salary increases or attractive offers from other firms.

Occasionally, the businessman's principal objective is a quiet life. He would rather have more leisure than a bigger profit; he prefers security and certainty[31] to bigger risks; he would rather be on good terms with his colleagues than have them as rivals. These are not hypothetical cases: they explain the economic decline of certain countries.

The need to have a ready supply of liquid assets often conflicts with the aim of maximizing profits: a firm will want to avoid contracting large debts and to keep its independence (preferring to finance investment from internal resources).

The exclusion of potential competition—as we have already noted —is not compatible with a policy designed to maximize profits either. Nor is the frequent case of a firm that is eager to maintain good relations with consumers, suppliers, investors, trade unions and in particular the government.

It has been pointed out that marginalism need not necessarily be

27 R. M. Cyert and J. G. March, *op. cit. supra* note 2.24, pp. 40–3.
28 W. J. Baumol, *Business behavior, value and growth* (New York 1959).
29 W. J. Baumol, 'On the theory of expansion of the firm', *The American Economic Review*, Dec 1962, p. 1085.
30 Cf. H. A. Simon, 'Theories of decision-making in economics and behavioral science', *The American Economic Review*, Jun 1959, p. 262.
31 Cf. G. Katona, *Psychological analysis of economic behavior* (New York 1951), p. 204. On the connection between market structure and certainty, see R. W. Clower, 'Some theory of an ignorant monopolist', *The Economic Journal*, Dec 1959.

linked with profit maximization.[32] It is possible—as W. Krelle[33] and others have shown—to use the marginal method to determine profit maximization at a given sales figure or sales maximization at a given profit. In each case, however, the problem is still a maximization problem (and the two are not really very different) being investigated by the same unreal methods.

It follows that the pursuit of maximum profit can no longer be considered the major objective of business activity; in our view the other objectives cannot even be regarded as subsidiary. The importance of these objectives differs from case to case, and general rules cannot be laid down.

Within the firm, its objectives are often the subject of fierce conflict among the various members of the staff, and the persuasiveness, tenacity or other qualities of one or other of them may clinch the matter. This in itself shows that the economic phenomenon cannot be studied by means of economics alone.

C. THE INSTRUMENTS OF MARKETING POLICY

Although it was soon pointed out that price is not the only instrument of marketing policy,[34] most attention is given to price in economic theory—as we stressed above. Often, however, price is of subordinate interest, and the other policy instruments such as quality, sales promotion and distribution systems are relied upon. These can, of course, influence price.

The extent to which the different instruments are used, i.e. what the marketing mix is, has not yet been examined very much.[35] We shall concentrate on the most important instruments. The choice of instruments depends first of all on the nature of the goods offered for sale. The financial situation may also be of great significance.[36]

32 E. Schneider, *op. cit. supra* note 2.16, p. 431.
33 W. Krelle, *Preistheorie* (Zürich 1961).
34 Cf. E. Schneider, 'Preistheorie oder Parametertheorie', *Weltwirtschaftliches Archiv*, 76/1 (1956), reprinted in *Volkswirtschaft und Betriebswirtschaft, op. cit. supra* note 2.16, p. 434.
35 H. B. Thorelli, 'The political economy of the firm: basis for a new theory of the firm', *Schweizerische Zeitschrift für Volkswirtschaft und Statistik*, 1965, Heft 3, p. 257.
36 N. Shubik, *Strategy and market structure. Competition, oligopoly and the theory of games* (New York 1959), pp. 35, 65, 71, 127, 134, 137.

1. Price

Price sensitivity varies from product to product. There are many goods (or types of good) for which the consumer pays little attention to price; on the other hand, there are others for which price is of great significance. And these goods or types of good differ from consumer to consumer.

Most consumers do little in the way of comparing prices—either for the same product at different times or for the same product on sale in different shops. They seem to remember only a limited number of prices.[37]

Price increases do not necessarily have a bad effect. They can be explained as being due to improved quality or greater demand. As a matter of fact, a number of firms make a systematic effort to market their product at a slightly higher price than their competitors' products. Knowing the reactions of numerous consumers, many firms attach a few unimportant gimmicks to their products and then sell them at a higher price than others.

Price reductions, on the other hand, are sometimes thought to signify a decline in quality, an unsuccessful line, difficulties in maintaining liquidity, or the imminent introduction of a new model. Even the price of a new product can be regarded as too low. When electric clocks were first marketed in the United States they were not successful. Consumers thought they were priced too low in comparison with the conventional clock; they felt that a quality product could not be sold at such a price. The clocks were withdrawn and later put on sale at a higher price—and this time with better results.[38]

2. Quality

This is a concept that can cover industrial design, packaging, servicing, delivery times and product variation. For many goods and services—dry cleaning, for instance—price is not as important as quality and speedy delivery.[39]

The quality of durable goods is often kept low deliberately in order to make them wear out sooner and thus promote replacement

---

37 H. Behrend, 'Price images, inflation and national incomes policy', *Scottish Journal of Political Economy*, Nov 1966.
38 A. R. Oxenfeldt, D. Miller, A. Shuchman and C. Winick, *op. cit. supra* note 1.20, p. 79.
39 See, e.g., 'Whiter laundries', *The Economist*, 10 Sep 1966, p. 1042.

purchases. When the consumer is accustomed to a price that is a good round figure, the quality (or the weight) is often reduced as an alternative to increasing the price (a practice known as product-line pricing).[40]

Packaging and servicing are becoming steadily more important. This also applies to product variation. By this we mean not the differentiation of a firm's products from those of its competitors but the way a firm makes temporary, minor changes in its own products in order to give the consumer the impression that new products are being brought out. This is a practice that causes considerable waste. In the United States at least $5000 million a year is spent on automobile model changes.[41] Small firms that cannot carry these costs go to the wall.[42]

3. Sales promotion
Sales promotion is the practice whereby firms employ representatives and advertising to inform dealers and consumers of the qualities of their products and to encourage them to buy. The word is used in its narrower sense here, since price and quality are also means of stimulating sales.

Marketing costs are only indirectly linked with the level of production; the figure differs from industry to industry. Huge amounts are spent on advertising in many industries. Annual expenditure on advertising in the United States totals about $22 000 million—the highest proportion on soap and other toiletries (15 per cent to 20 per cent) and on cigarettes and alcohol (about 10 per cent of cost price).

Advertising, in addition to its useful function of providing information, can force prices up. In many cases advertising does not increase a firm's market share because it is 'retaliatory, competitive and self-cancelling'.[43] The two biggest soap producers in the United Kingdom, Lever Bros and Procter & Gamble, realized this and decided in 1961 on a voluntary cutback in advertising expenditure.

---

40 J. Dean, 'Problems of product-line pricing', *Journal of Marketing*, Jan 1950.
41 Not to mention the increased cost of petrol consumption (about $7000 million) : F. M. Fisher, Z. Griliches and C. Kaysen, 'The costs of automobile changes since 1949', *The American Economic Review*, May 1962. Cf. J. S. Bain, *Price theory* (New York 1952), p. 332.
42 J. A. Menge, 'Style change costs as a market weapon', *The Quarterly Journal of Economics*, Nov 1962.
43 J. Weinrich, 'Workable competition and the L-shaped cost curve', *Rivista Internazionale di Scienze Economiche e Commerciali*, Jul 1965, p. 686.

This was followed by a price cut.[44] Nevertheless, the agreement did not last, mainly because of 'the uncertainties in the minds of each company about the competitive intentions of the other, particularly with regard to new products'. Moreover, it was thought that a powerful newcomer to the industry might mount major advertising campaigns for his products.[45]

Firms are often put out of business by competitors whose products are inferior (or whose production facilities are not as good) but who put a bigger effort into sales promotion.[46]

Excessive advertising uses up funds that could be employed for productive purposes. This explains K. D. Jacob's view that, as far as fulfilling the macroeconomic functions of competition is concerned, competition in advertising is virtually useless.[47]

It is not easy, however, to determine when advertising takes on excessive proportions, particularly as it has not yet been studied scientifically.[48]

Here we may recall the statement attributed to the first Lord Leverhulme: 'I realize that one half of the money I spend in advertising is wasted. The trouble is, no one can tell me which half.'

4. Distribution

A firm can see to the distribution of its own products or can give the job to outsiders. Which is best will vary from industry to industry. The drawback to independent dealers—who have to be used in many cases—is that competition between producers of goods with fixed retail prices often leads to higher margins and prices. For a shopkeeper will naturally encourage purchases of the products on which he earns most. Even apart from competition of this kind, margins are often 'far greater than efficient retailers require'.[49] The same holds good for importers' and wholesalers' margins.

Firms are often obliged to extend their range so as to have a

---

44 *Prices of household and toilet soaps, soap powders and soap flakes, and soapless detergents* (National Board for Prices and Incomes, Report No. 4 Cmnd 2791, London 1965), p. 14.

45 *Ibid.*, p. 15.

46 A. R. Oxenfeldt, *Marketing practices in the TV set industry* (New York 1964), p. 247.

47 K. D. Jacob, 'Werbung und Wettbewerb: eine theoretische Analyse', *Schmollers Jahrbuch für Gesetzgebung, Verwaltung und Volkswirtschaft* 1966, Heft 4, p. 420.

48 Cf. D. C. Hague, *supra* note 2.20, p. 9. J. S. Bain, *op. cit. supra* note 2.41, p. 450, wonders whether ruling out excessive marketing cost would be compatible with a free-enterprise system.

49 S. H. Slichter, 'The growth of competition', *The Atlantic Monthly*, Nov 1953, cited in *Potentials of the American economy. Selected essays of Sumner H. Slichter* (ed. J. T. Dunlop, Cambridge, Mass., 1961), p. 36.

better negotiating position with dealers. Direct costing may provide pointers as regards policy on this matter.

D. CONCLUSIONS

The conclusions to be drawn from the foregoing relate to the current theory's lack of touch with reality, the likelihood of any new theory being constructed, the nature of analysis technique, the need to refer to other sciences and the changes in observers' views of the function of the firm.

1. The unreality of marginalist theory

The *Methodenstreit* that flared up between marginalists and anti-marginalists after the last World War[50] put the former increasingly on the defensive. In 1967 Machlup admits that 'some anti-marginalist suggestions have led in recent years to a number of revisions in the marginal analysis of the firm'.[51] He also believes that there has been a marriage of sorts between marginalism and managerialism.[52]

In fact, he adds, managerialism is better able to supply answers, particularly those of an advisory nature, to questions concerning specific firms.[53]

However, as we have said, these modified views are still not reflected sufficiently in the theory as generally taught, where profit maximization and price remain the matters of importance. All other factors are assumed to be constant. The marginalists forget how slippery a tool[54] the *ceteris paribus* clause is.

Theoretical economics ought to fit reality as closely as possible. Consequently, it must regularly be adjusted to changed circumstances. This is the only way in which it can form a basis for economic policy.[55]

50 See mainly R. A. Lester, 'Shortcomings of marginal analysis for wage-employment problems', *The American Economic Review*, Mar 1946; F. Machlup, *supra* note 2.17. For critical observations on Machlup's views, see, e.g., H. A. J. F. Misset, 'Het producentengedrag en het marginalisme', *De Economist*, Sep–Oct 1966, p. 500.
51 F. Machlup, *supra* note 2.21, p. 4.
52 *Ibid.*, p. 29.
53 *Ibid.*, p. 31.
54 A. Burns, *The frontiers of economic research* (Princeton 1954), p. 8.
55 Cf. H. G. Moulton, 'Some comments on research method', in *Economic research in the development of economic science and public policy* (Washington 1946), p. 52.

There is no such link with reality in the current theory of price, so it should not come as a surprise to learn that there is 'no empirical basis to the axioms of the neoclassical theory of rational economic behaviour',[56] and D. Schneider is right to ask whether business economics should concern itself at all with current price theory.[57]

The marginalist theory of price can never produce a standard for firms to go by.[58] But if we take it that it is incorrect to regard the marginal principle as normative,[59] then we can only deplore the intellectual effort that has been expended on marginalism without any practical end in view. As R. Miry noted in another context, we have no use for strictly logical conclusions about an equilibrium that never occurs in reality, nor for clear-cut formulas worked out in the ivory towers where, as O. Morgenstern once put it, scholars pass their time trying 'to suck the factual world out of their finger-tips'.[60]

D. C. Hague, not without reason, has said: 'For far too long, we have been content to pass on to our students myth rather than fact about price and price policy simply because we have not known what the facts were.'[61] The need for more empirical research in the field of price determination has therefore been given repeated emphasis.

2. Towards a new theory of prices?

The anti-marginalists have often been accused of demolishing one theory without having another to put up in its place. This is partly true but is no reason for leaving an unsatisfactory doctrine intact.[62]

Discussions on this point are still in full swing. If a more realistic theory can be constructed, it will certainly be a more complex one. This should not surprise us. Innumerable factors influence price

56 G. Kade, *Die Grundlagen der Preistheorie. Eine Kritik an den Ausgangssätzen der mikroökono-mischen Modellbildung* (Berlin 1962), p. 159; a rejoinder (with a defence of neoclassical price theory) can be found in G. Ollenburg, 'Preistheorie und Methodenkritik. Zu Kades Buch: "Die Grundannahmen der Preistheorie"', *Finanzarchiv* 1966, Bd. 25, Heft 2.
57 D. Schneider, 'Die Preis-Absatz-Funktion und das Dilemma der Preistheorie', *Zeitschrift für die gesamte Staatswissenschaft*, Oct 1966, p. 606.
58 H. A. J. F. Misset, *supra* note 2.50, p. 500.
59 J. E. Andriessen, *De ontwikkeling van de moderne prijstheorie* (3rd edn, revised by A. Heertje, Leiden 1965), p. 133.
60 R. Miry, 'Vraagtekens en tekortkomingen', *Tijdschrift voor Economie en Sociologie*, Oct 1937, p. 368.
61 D. C. Hague, *supra* note 2.20, p. 9.
62 Cf. H. A. Simon, *supra* note 2.30, p. 280: 'The sketchiness and incompleteness of the newer proposals has been urged as a compelling reason for clinging to the older theories, however inadequate they are admitted to be.'

determination. Price often plays no part in a firm's marketing policy. There seems to be virtually no possibility of establishing general rules here. As A. R. Oxenfeldt has remarked, 'The detailed analysis of prices ... suggests that every price is unique in some important respect. No fairly simple explanation of price, like the law of supply and demand, has been uncovered ... There seems to be far too much diversity of business circumstances for individual businessmen to rely on some simple pricing rule to carry them through'.[63]

'Pricing is more an art than a science', another writer believes.[64] 'It is the result of an attempt to balance factors to which no precise weight can be attached. The problem is not mathematical, but rather one of estimating the effects of various marketing policies upon sales—both in the near and distant future. Because of variations in a thousand and one factors, what is good policy for one company may be unworkable for another.'

Similar points have been made about other economic phenomena. On the theory of international trade, J. Viner emphasizes that 'The world has changed greatly, and is now a world of planned economies, of state trading, of substantially arbitrary and flexible national price structures, and of managed instability in exchange rates. The classical theory is not directly relevant for such a world, and it may be that for such a world there is and can be no relevant *general* theory'.[65] And, according to J. Williams, 'International trade is so complex, so subject to heterogeneous conditions and to ceaseless changes in conditions that it seems to me almost naïve to speak of the theory of international trade'.[66]

In connection with other matters again, it has been established that current theory can neither explain what has happened nor forecast what will happen. As D. B. J. Schouten puts it, we are forced by the uncertainties of economic life to adopt a pragmatic approach; we must not look for laws of motion or for conformity to any such laws but simply take steps to attain our aims.[67] Without going so far as to assert that no laws should be looked for, we must

63 A. R. Oxenfeldt, *op. cit. supra* note 2.23, p. 577.
64 N. K. Dhalla, 'The art of product pricing', *Management Review*, Jun 1964, p. 65, cited in D. V. Harper, *op. cit. supra* note 2.23, p. 295.
65 J. Viner, *International economics* (Glencoe 1951), p. 16.
66 J. Williams, 'International trade and policy. Some current issues', *The American Economic Review*, May 1951, p. 420.
67 D. B. J. Schouten, 'Het systeem van Goudriaan', *Tijdschrift Economie*, Sep 1952, p. 577.

admit that attempts to track them down have led to much dis-
illusionment. We must resign ourselves to the fact that economics
does not have all the answers but is first and foremost a method, or
—in the somewhat exaggerated words of Lord Keynes—'a method
rather than a doctrine, an apparatus of the mind, a technique of
thinking'.[68]

In no case—and this applies to marginalist price theory above
all—should economics be a matter of blind faith with no links with
reality. Nevertheless, we must expect that 'some marginalists will
continue to clutch the theory to their breasts, even though it be a
mere figment they hold'.[69]

To our way of thinking, what Joan Robinson wrote in 1947 still
holds good: 'It occurs that economic science has not yet solved its
first problem—what determines the price of a commodity?'[70]

3. The nature of analysis technique

Mathematics can be a useful aid in explaining economic problems
provided the user is aware of its limitations. But there is little point
in employing the most refined mathematical techniques for analysing
problems—such as pricing in oligopolies—that are so complex and
in which so many uneconomic factors must be taken into account.

Nevertheless, far too many economists assume 'naïvely but arro-
gantly . . . all too readily the applicability to the real world of
the beautiful theoretical models which they use in their researches'.[71]
They are, as G. L. S. Shackle rightly says, 'totally unconscious that
their reasonings cannot, at one and the same time, be rigorous and
yet capable of seizing all the essentials of reality'.[72]

The dangers of the mathematical method have been brought
out repeatedly by, for instance, G. Pirou, who pointed out that
the long series of learned equations drawn up by mathematician
economists have so far 'revealed no new truth nor anything that
cannot be written down in ordinary language',[73] and by A. Marchal,
who deplores the attitude that considers the construction of a mathematical model an end rather than a means and fails to distinguish

68 J. M. Keynes, Introduction to the *Cambridge Economic Handbooks.*
69 B. B. Seligman, *Main currents in modern economics. Economic thought since 1870* (New York
    1962), p. 366.
70 J. Robinson, *An essay on Marxian economics* (London 1947), p. 79.
71 E. Devons, 'Economists and the public', *Lloyds Bank Review,* Jul 1965, p. 22.
72 G. L. S. Shackle, reviewing N. Georgescu-Roegen, *Analytical economics. Issues and problems,*
    in *The Economic Journal,* Dec 1967, p. 859.
73 G. Pirou, *La valeur et les prix* (Paris 1948), p. 129.

the mathematical solution from the solution that is humanly and politically practical.[74]

However, over the last twenty years economic science has been going further in the wrong direction, and in the economic journals we find more useless mental gymnastics than economics. This is particularly true of price theory. In discussing the theory of monopolistic competition, L. Robbins puts it this way: 'For all the proliferation of diagrams in recent literature, I doubt whether, analytically, we have advanced very far beyond Marshall's few lines of algebra; and I suspect that in practical judgment and sense of proportion, we are often some way behind.'[75]

4. The other sciences

The complexity of price determination is making economists increasingly aware that they must call on other disciplines such as sociology and psychology.[76] Economics cannot ignore the political and social circumstances in which economic activity unfolds.

Economics may be said to examine the whole range of human behaviour from a specific angle. K. Boulding goes so far as to admit: 'I have been gradually coming under the conviction, disturbing for a professional theorist, that there is no such thing as economics— there is only social science applied to economic problems'.[77]

In any case, the economist will always have to rely upon other sciences. We agree with C. P. Kindleberger that if the economist is not prepared to study certain political and social conditions, alone or with representatives of other disciplines, he must give up all idea of explaining economic phenomena or even of giving advice on economic policy, except within very narrow limits.[78]

5. The function of the firm

As we have seen, various interests have to be taken into account when a firm sets its prices—the interests of consumers, suppliers,

74 A. Marchal, *Méthode scientifique et science économique, tome I: Le conflit traditionnel des méthodes et son renouvellement* (Paris 1952), p. 79. See also A. Lowe, *On economic knowledge. Toward a science of political economics* (New York 1965), p. 5, and the review by H. Wilhelm, 'Instrumentale Wirtschaftstheorie und rationelle Wirtschaftspolitik. Gedanken zu einem Buch von Adolphe Lowe', *Zeitschrift für die gesamte Staatswissenschaft*, Jul 1967.
75 L. Robbins, 'The economist in the twentieth century', *Economica*, May 1949, p. 97.
76 Cf., e.g., G. L. S. Shackle, *Uncertainty in economics and other reflexions* (Cambridge 1955), p. 241 ; J. M. Buchanan, 'Economics and its scientific neighbours', in *The structure of economic science. Essays on methodology* (ed. S. R. Krupp, Englewood Cliffs 1966), p. 8.
77 K. E. Boulding, *A reconstruction of economics* (2nd edn, New York 1962), p. vii.
78 C. P. Kindleberger, Introduction to M. Moret, *L'échange international* (Paris 1957), p. 18.

middlemen, competitors and not least the government. And, as we have also noted, the price is often determined as a result of discussions within the firm between the heads of different departments.[79]

Firms are in fact showing increasing awareness of their social responsibility. If necessary, the task of government must be 'to make the firm more aware of its responsibility towards the people it employs and the people among whom it lives'.[80]

Hence, some writers believe that the firm should no longer be seen as an institution bent on making a profit but as 'a political community of internal and external interest groups'[81]—consumers, management and staff, shareholders and other creditors, suppliers, distributors, competitors, government. Indeed the divergent interests of which the firm has to take account explain the various objectives that we have been discussing.

If we accept this view, it is no longer a matter of indifference how a firm is managed. We should perhaps ask ourselves whether the necessary skills should not be required of the leaders of big business, particularly when positions of leadership are passed on from father to son.[82] But all too often the decline of firms can be put down to lethargic and inefficient management. For instance, waste of resources contributes to unnecessary price increases. The firm and its management must be seen henceforth in the context of altered economic and social circumstances.

79 A. R. Oxenfeldt, *Executive action in marketing* (Belmont, Cal., 1967), Chapter 10.
80 F. Bloch-Lainé, *Pour une réforme de l'entreprise* (Paris 1963), p. 129.
81 H. B. Thorelli, *supra* note 2.35, p. 249.
82 F. Bloch-Lainé, *op. cit. supra* note 2.80, p. 151.

3 The instruments of price policy

As depressions, and even recessions, become rarer, price policy is called upon to play a greater part in economic policy in general. In the following chapter we shall deal with the various instruments of price policy. This constitutes no more than a general survey, but it nevertheless needs to be preceded by a statement of the aims of economic policy, in particular price stability, and the causes of price increases. The survey will be rounded off by a few conclusions.

A. AIMS OF ECONOMIC POLICY

In the traditional concept, the goal pursued in economic policy is maximum production. According to economic philosophy, account must also be taken of non-economic aims. Finally, present-day thinking maintains that the aims of economic policy must not be determined by economic theory. This is a task for governments,[1] and it is not for the theory of economic policy to adopt any standpoint regarding such aims. What it does is to indicate the means[2] to achieve them.

Where any aspect of public policy—e.g. defence policy or social policy—involves drawing upon available resources, it must be taken into consideration in economic policy. This means that economic policy concerns itself with the economic aspects of overall policy.

1 Although the activity of households and enterprises may contribute to the fulfilment of objectives, the general view is that economic policy is solely the province of the public authorities.
2 Non-intervention may also be considered such a means.

With due regard to the priorities laid down by the government, it endeavours to use the available resources to the best possible advantage.

Every economist can, of course, champion his own ideas in the field of economic aims.[3] The main objectives of economic policy are generally considered to be:[4]

a. economic expansion, or stepping up the *per capita* national product,[5] which involves combating cyclical fluctuations and optimum use of the factors of production
b. equitable distribution of the national income, which means achieving full employment.

In point of fact, it is difficult to segregate these two objectives; heavy unemployment or unbalanced distribution have repercussions on demand, and hence on supply. Even so, economic expansion does not necessarily bring about better distribution.

These major aims are usually supplemented by secondary ones. Among the latter are the protection of specific industries, the maintenance of gold and foreign currency reserves and aid to certain social classes.[6] These secondary aims are invariably comprised in the major objectives. The betterment of underprivileged population groups, for example, should in the normal course be achieved by equitable distribution of income. Objectives such as peace[7] or freedom[8] appear to us to fall within the scope of overall policy and not of economic policy.

What is frequently forgotten is the need to examine the compatibility of these secondary aims and to fix an order of priority.[9] Similarly, the distinction between instruments and aims of economic policy is sometimes overlooked.

3 Except that if he is a civil servant, he must not dispute, but must contribute to the fulfilment of the government's directives.
4 Cf. M. A. G. van Meerhaeghe, *op. cit. supra* note 1.1, pp. 394–5.
5 A better basis would be the trend of productivity, since this takes account of changes in the number of hours worked and the ratio between the working and the total population. However, calculation of such productivity gives rise to still more difficulties.
6 J. Tinbergen, *Economic policy: principles and design* (Amsterdam 1956), p. 16.
7 *Ibid.*, p. 15.
8 K. E. Boulding, *Principles of economic policy* (Englewood Cliffs 1958), pp. 19, 110.
9 Cf. T. Pütz, *Theorie der allgemeinen Wirtschaftspolitik und Wirtschaftslenkung* (Vienna 1948), p. 10; P. Hennipman, 'Doeleinden en criteria der economische politiek', in *Theorie van de economische politiek. Een systematisch overzicht met bijdragen van Belgische en Nederlandse auteurs* (eds. J. E. Andriessen and M. A. G. van Meerhaeghe, Leiden 1962), p. 75; M. A. G. van Meerhaeghe, 'De doeleinden van de economische politiek. De objectieven volgens de Belgische regeringsverklaringen', *Tijdschrift voor Sociale Wetenschappen*, 1962 No. 2.

B. PRICE STABILITY

Price stability,[10] or monetary equilibrium, is more a means than an end, since it makes for both better income distribution and increased production. It is mainly in periods of prosperity that it becomes an aim of governments. Other forms of economic policy are then subordinated to it; prosperity frequently finds expression in an upthrust of prices, which brings with it many drawbacks.

Inflation, or the non-stop rise in the overall level of prices of consumer goods,[11] places fixed-income groups and creditors at a disadvantage[12]: 'invisible thieves' are at work.[13] Systems linking wages to the index would at first sight appear to afford a means of protection (although there is a time-lag in the adjustment process). In point of fact, they decrease the flexibility of the economy and contribute to the inflationary tendencies. If this method is adopted, moreover, it should be extended to all income, which is far from being the case at the present time. When W. B. Reddaway contends that inflation is not so tragic because real incomes also rise,[14] he loses sight of just such groups as these.

Inflation has the effect of discouraging certain investments (bonds, savings books) and may therefore hamper capital formation. Finally, in the absence of corresponding inflation in other countries, it slows down exports and leads either to an alteration of the exchange rate or to quotas. Increases in prices aggravate economic fluctuations.

While 'galloping' inflation is condemned by all, many authors defend 'creeping' inflation because they claim that it stimulates economic growth;[15] the resultant increase in profits, for instance, brings about an expansion in investment.

10 The stability of a single price index is not the only criterion. Other factors have to be taken into consideration: *The problem of rising prices* (OEEC, Paris 1961), p. 11. Price indices as such do not allow for improvement in quality and the introduction of new products on the market. See *Economic report of the President transmitted to the Congress January 1964 together with the annual report of the Council of Economic Advisers* (Washington 1964), p. 35.

11 M. A. G. van Meerhaeghe, *op. cit. supra* note 1.1, p. 276. For an outline of the various definitions of inflation, see W. G. Bowen, *The wage-price issue. A theoretical analysis* (Princeton 1960), pp. 15–33. As regards the difficulties of measuring this 'overall' level, see M. Bronfenbrenner and F. D. Holzman, 'Survey of inflation theory', *The American Economic Review,* Sep 1963.

12 Cf. G. L. Bach and A. Ando, 'The redistributional effects of inflation', *The Review of Economics and Statistics,* Feb 1957 ; M. Bronfenbrenner and F. D. Holzman, *supra* note 3.11, pp. 646–52.

13 E. Küng, 'Das Eigentum im Spannungsfeld der Kräfte von Wirtschaft und Gesellschaft', in U. Scheuner and E. Küng, *Der Schutz des Eigentums, Untersuchungen zu Artikel 14 des Grundgesetzes für die Bundesrepublik Deutschland* (Hannover n.d.), p. 52.

14 W. B. Reddaway, 'Rising prices for ever?', *Lloyds Bank Review,* Jul 1966.

15 See, e.g., S. H. Slichter, 'Statement', in *Employment, growth and price levels, op. cit. supra* note 1.28; W. L. Thorp and R. E. Quandt, *The new inflation* (New York 1959), p. 227 ;

Moderate inflation, however, is in no way essential to economic growth,[16] which has frequently been more marked in periods of stability. During periods of prosperity it is not the countries where inflation is heaviest which necessarily record the most progress.[17] A slight degree of inflation fosters speculative investments in particular.[18] The growth which it generates will be 'subject to shocks and interruptions'.[19] One of the chief aims of economic policy in the less-developed countries 'should be to maintain price stability, otherwise the objective of economic growth will be jeopardized'.[20]

Similar observations may be made concerning the relation between full employment and inflation. The simultaneous achievement of price stability and full employment is difficult, but these two objectives are not incompatible as many authors claim.[21]

Another argument is sometimes advanced in favour of a slight degree of inflation.[22] This is that it smooths relations between employers and trade unions; the former's opposition to wage increases is less marked when prices are rising steadily. As for the trade unions, their members always appreciate an improvement in their wages— which they attribute to their own campaigning—even if in real terms their income remains unchanged. Trade-union leaders are, however, becoming increasingly aware of the chimerical nature of such 'victories'.

Inflation is neither desirable nor 'inevitable'.[23] Rather is it that

---

E. S. Kirschen and L. Morissens, 'Les objectifs de la politique économique', *Cahiers économiques de Bruxelles*, Feb 1960, p. 164 ; F. Hartog, 'Leven met kruipende inflatie', *Maandschrift Economie*, Aug 1964, p. 515.

16 G. Bombach, 'Quantitative und monetäre Aspekte des Wirtschaftswachstums', in *Finanz- und währungspolitische Bedingungen stetigen Wirtschaftswachstums. Schriften des Vereins für Sozialpolitik* (Berlin 1959), p. 201 ; U. Tun Wai, 'The relation between inflation and economic development', *International Monetary Fund Staff Papers*, Oct 1959 ; G. S. Dorrance, 'The effect of inflation on economic development', *International Monetary Fund Staff Papers*, Mar 1963.

17 Cf. A. W. Marget, 'Inflation : some lessons of recent foreign exchange', *The American Economic Review*, May 1960; R. J. Bhatia, 'Inflation, deflation and economic development', *International Monetary Fund Staff Papers*, Nov 1960.

18 Cf. *First report* (Council on Prices, Productivity and Incomes, London 1958), p. 52 : '... even ... a slow rise does great injustice between different sections of the population, and if it were generally expected to continue indefinitely would hamper many kinds of business dealings, including long-term borrowing by Government.'

19 *The problem of rising prices, op. cit. supra* note 3.10, p. 11.

20 P. K. Mitra, 'Inflazione e sviluppo economico', *Rivista Internazionale di Scienze Economiche e Commerciali*, Jul 1966, p. 655.

21 See, e.g., S. H. Slichter, *supra* note 3.15 ; P. A. Samuelson and R. M. Solow, 'Analytical aspects of anti-inflation policy', *The American Economic Review*, May 1960, pp. 191–4 ; H. Scherf, *Untersuchungen zur Theorie der Inflation* (Kieler Studien, Tübingen 1967), p. 113.

22 K. E. Boulding, *op. cit. supra* note 3.8, pp. 59, 154.

23 E. S. Kirschen and L. Morissens, *supra* note 3.15, p. 58. See also the fatalistic views held by *The Economist*, 8 Oct 1966, pp. 169–70.

governments do not attach sufficient importance to price stability[24] and do not take steps—frequently unpopular—needed to ensure it.

The blame for this is shared by all political parties and it just will not do to ascribe inflationary sympathies to one in particular, as the liberal writer D. Villey does to the socialists, who in his view are 'congenitally indulgent towards inflation'.[25] Socialists are as well aware as others that the inflationary spiral 'in the end always favours the haves at the expense of the have-nots'.[26]

This lack of determination on the part of the public authorities prompts consumers and producers to anticipate fresh rises in prices.[27] Consumption increases and the inflationary trend gathers momentum.

C. CAUSES OF PRICE RISES

The causes[28] of inflation are generally held to be either excess demand or cost increases. Frequently, too, exceptional or temporary factors are adduced, as are administered prices.

It is difficult to pinpoint the cause or causes of inflation. If excess demand is in many cases regarded as the main cause, its significance differs considerably from country to country or from period to period. The interdependence of the various causes is not calculated to facilitate examination of the phenomenon; this, however, is essential in view of the pointers which it can provide as regards stabilization policy.[29]

Whatever the cause of inflation, it is invariably accompanied by an expansion of the money supply.[30]

---

24 J. Åkerman, 'An institutional approach to the problem of inflation', in *Stabile Preise in wachsender Wirtschaft. Das Inflationsproblem. Erich Schneider zum 60. Geburtstag* (ed. G. Bombach, Tübingen 1960), pp. 6–8.

25 D. Villey, '*Jacques Rueff, un libéral moderne*', in *Fondements philosophiques des systèmes économiques. Textes de Jacques Rueff de l'Académie française et textes rédigés en son honneur* (ed. E. M. Claassen, Paris 1967), p. 165.

26 C. Bruclain, *Le socialisme et l'Europe* (Paris 1965), p. 34.

27 According to G. Katona, this preoccupation is less pronounced in the United States (*The powerful consumer. Psychological studies of the American economy*, New York 1960, p. 208). This is certainly no longer the case at the present time.

28 W. G. Bowen, *op. cit. supra* note 3.11, p. 415, prefers to speak of 'origins'.

29 Cf. M. Fleming, 'Cost-induced inflation and the quantity theory of money', *The Economic Journal*, Sep 1961, pp. 519–20; A. J. Hagger, 'Inflation types', *Economia Internazionale*, May 1964, p. 224.

30 E. Despres, M. Milton, A. G. Hart, P. A. Samuelson and D. H. Wallace, 'The problem of economic instability: a committee report', *The American Economic Review*, Sep 1950, p. 510; G. Haberler, *Inflation. Its causes and cures. Revised and enlarged edition with a new look at inflation in 1966* (Washington 1967), pp. 63, 77.

1. Excess demand

Excess demand is imputable to either the industrial sector (with planned investment exceeding anticipated savings), the public authorities ('budgetary inflation') or external relations (balance-of-payments surplus).

In the normal course, equilibrium is restored by a rise in prices; with production facilities being used to capacity, employers endeavour—by offering higher wages, for instance—to lure manpower away from other firms and other industries.[31]

It is not certain, however, that prices will rise straight away, at least in the case of manufactured goods; as long as costs do not undergo any changes, administered prices are frequently held down. In consequence, inflation sometimes does not make itself felt until some months of excess demand have elapsed.

At the outset, the pressure of demand is not exerted in all industries. Especially when its pattern alters considerably, as was the case in the immediate post-war period,[32] demand is concentrated in the basic industries (such as steel). Here the upward movement of prices may originate, even if in other industries there are reserves of manpower; it frequently happens that the workers in question lack the proper skills or are not prepared to undertake the travelling involved.

2. Cost increases

a. Wages

By bidding against each other as they do, employers bring about rises in wages, and consequently in production costs and prices too. As we have just pointed out, the movement may be triggered off by a single industry, more often than not one with high productivity and a monopolistic position. From this trade unions will obtain more advantages without the increase in wages necessarily outstripping the growth in productivity. Workers in other industries will not, however, countenance too pronounced a lag in their incomes compared with others; this will generate increases in wages higher than those in productivity, and also rises in prices.

In a word, the trade unions take advantage of excess demand to

---

31 Cf. B. Hansen, *A study in the theory of inflation* (London 1951).
32 *National and international measures for full employment* (United Nations, New York 1949), p. 44.

press their wage claims. This has the effect of accelerating the inflation caused by the disparity between supply and demand.

It is, however, possible for wage increases to be autonomous, in which case they give rise to what is called cost-push inflation. They occur in periods of stability or recession, always provided that the increase in wages exceeds that in productivity. It is a mistake to use this proviso as a definition of cost-push inflation: a faster rate of increase such as this may also be found where demand-pull inflation prevails.[33]

b. Other factors

Cost-push inflation may also be caused by a rise in prices of (imported) raw materials, or in general by a rise in prices of imported products, or by increases in distribution costs, taxes or profits.

c. Administered prices

It is mainly firms holding a monopolistic or oligopolistic position which are able to increase profit margins. In industries where such situations obtain, competition is based more on presentation and advertising than on prices. Administered prices are not changed very often—usually after a wage rise.[34] The opportunity is taken to increase profit margins. The latter may also be stepped up as a result of advances in productivity which do not find expression in a fall in prices. Decreases in production costs have only partial repercussions.

The asymmetrical behaviour of administered prices hampers efforts to stabilize the overall price level, for increases in prices are now scarcely ever offset by price cuts in high-productivity industries.[35]

The existence of other restrictive practices and of guaranteed price systems in agriculture is not sufficient justification for minimizing the inflationary danger from industrial monopolies and oligopolies.[36]

While 'the raising ... is necessarily limited ... to a few industries' (there is no 'profits round'),[37] the increase in prices resulting from a stepping-up of the profit margin in some basic industries may nevertheless lie at the root of an inflationary movement.

33 P. A. Samuelson and R. M. Solow, *supra* note 3.21, p. 182.
34 Moreover, the trade unions obtain wage increases more easily in the firms in question. See in particular F. W. Rutten, *Prijsvorming in de industrie* (Leiden 1965), p. 178.
35 *The problem of rising prices, op. cit. supra* note 3.10, p. 71. G. Haberler, however, considers that the rigidity of wages is still more pronounced than that of monopolistic prices (*op. cit. supra* note 3.30, p. 73).
36 As G. Haberler does, *op. cit. supra* note 3.30, p. 76.
37 *The problem of rising prices, op. cit. supra* note 3.10, p. 70.

The government's price policy would be facilitated if there were a better knowledge of the principles underlying industrial price policy.[38] In this respect, the literature shows a regrettable lacuna. The same applies as regards the operation of markets, both domestic[39] and international.[40]

3. Exceptional or temporary factors

Among the factors of special origin which tend to cause rises in prices are:[41]

a. the adjustment of controlled prices, e.g. rent increases, abolition of subsidies
b. the raising of indirect taxes and customs duties
c. variations in the quality of goods
d. fortuitous occurrences (e.g. a crop failure, an international crisis)
e. changes in import and export prices as a result of external circumstances.

These causes of price increases are, in fact, no more than special cases of cost-push inflation factors (the first three, sometimes the last) and demand-pull inflation factors (the fourth, sometimes the last).

D. INSTRUMENTS OF PRICE POLICY

Inflation has generated a 'torrent of literature',[42] which is 'virtually no longer assimilable'.[43] Most of it relates to the instruments for combating inflation.

In Western countries, the chief instruments of price policy are fiscal policy, monetary policy, wages and incomes policy, competition policy and policy in the field of international economic relations. In addition, there are certain forms of direct action.

---

38 M. A. G. van Meerhaeghe, *op. cit. supra* note 1.13, p. 249 ; T. Beste, 'Möglichkeiten und Grenzen der Preispolitik in der Unternehmung', *Zeitschrift für betriebswirtschaftliche Forschung*, Mar 1964, p. 143.
39 M. A. G. van Meerhaeghe, *op. cit. supra* note 1.13, p. 311.
40 J. Houssiaux, 'International trade and antitrust regulations : a European viewpoint', *Economia Internazionale*, Aug 1966, p. 455.
41 *The problem of rising prices, op. cit. supra* note 3.10, pp. 26–7.
42 G. Haberler, *op. cit. supra* note 3.30, p. 45.
43 G. Bombach, *supra* note 3.16, p. 190.

1. Fiscal policy

The authorities influence demand not only through revenue but also through expenditure. Like monetary policy, policy on government revenue and expenditure is one of the essential weapons in the fight against inflation, especially when the latter is caused by excess demand.

Where price increases are due to exceptional or temporary factors, a subsidy policy may help to avoid an inflationary spiral. To maintain that 'a special price rise ought not to constitute grounds for an upward movement of wages and salaries'[44] is to show little appreciation of the facts. The problem is to avoid special price increases by taking appropriate steps.

At first sight, tax policy would appear likely to achieve better results than monetary policy. In practice, governments do not avail themselves of it to any great extent, not so much because of technical difficulties—many items of expenditure are incompressible and alteration of tax rates involves protracted discussion in Parliament—as because of political factors. It is feared that the electorate will remember a tax increase longer than a moderate rise in the overall price level.

The business sector too is usually against, even necessary, deflationary measures. Hence Lord Robbins's pronouncement that 'the majority of businessmen are inflationists'.[45]

2. Monetary policy

In order to have any chance of succeeding, monetary policy—like fiscal policy, for that matter—must be conducted with promptitude and firmness.[46] An unduly restrictive policy, however, must be avoided, since it has more effect on production than on prices. It is less appropriate in the case of cost-push inflation.

Wielding the instruments of monetary policy is not easy. It is impossible to gauge to a nicety the consequences of open-market operations, of raising Bank Rate or of other measures aimed at restricting credit, whether for production or for consumption.[47] As regards the possibilities offered by monetary policy, E. Lundberg

44 *The problem of rising prices, op. cit. supra* note 3.10, p. 31.
45 Lord Robbins, 'An economist looks at business', in J. Jewkes, Sir Paul Chambers and Lord Robbins, *Economics, business and government* (Institute of Economic Affairs, London 1966), p. 31.
46 Cf. *The problem of rising prices, op. cit. supra* note 3.10, p. 39.
47 M. A. G. van Meerhaeghe, *op. cit. supra* note 1.1, p. 412.

has coined the expression 'well-informed uncertainty'.[48] Although monetary policy still claims its champions,[49] many authors have misgivings as to its efficiency.[50]

Selective measures are at all events necessary in cases of inflation induced by excess demand in a basic industry (e.g. metallurgy or construction). Frequently, too, a certain degree of discrimination is desirable because powerful firms (those with a monopolistic or oligopolistic position) are the last to be affected by monetary policy. This prompts the following observation from J. K. Galbraith: '. . . we shall be increasingly faced with the choice between inflation or highly discriminatory . . . measures for contending with it'.[51]

The fact is that the members of an economic union, which the countries in the European Economic Community are now constructing, are no longer free agents in the choice of instruments of monetary policy. An autonomous policy, taking no account of measures enacted in other member countries, would endanger the free movement of goods and capital.

3. Incomes policy

Inflation caused or accelerated by cost increases can be obviated by intervening at the income-determination stage.[52] As we have already pointed out, monetary policy will not be so effective in this case.

There is general agreement that the average increase in wages—those actually paid out, not the agreed rates—must not exceed the average rise in productivity. This principle can be applied either on a macroecomonic scale or by industry or enterprise.[53]

If all wages follow the trend of the country's average productivity, those industries in which the productivity increase has been above the average will have an advantage. In other industries, prices will

48 E. Lundberg, 'The possibilities of monetary policy', *Quarterly Review Skandinaviska Banken*, Oct 1961, p. 99.
49 See in particular J. R. Schlesinger, 'Monetary policy and its critics', *The Journal of Political Economy*, Dec 1960; G. Macesich, 'Tre punti di vista sull'inflazione: retrospettiva del "Grande dibattito"', *Rivista Internazionale di Scienze Economiche e Commerciali*, May 1964.
50 See, e.g., W. G. Bowen, *op. cit. supra* note 3.11, p. 371. Cf. the report of a correspondent of *The Economist*, 26 Nov 1966, p. xi: 'on a failure of traditional monetary policy when it has to act under conditions where fiscal policy was not backing it up'.
51 J. K. Galbraith, 'Market structure and stabilization policy', *The Review of Economics and Statistics*, Mar 1957, p. 133.
52 Needless to say, price changes must also reflect variations in non-wage costs.
53 See on this subject J. Lecaillon, 'La politique des revenus', *Revue d'Economie Politique*, May–Jun 1965; H. A. Turner and H. Zoeteweij, *Prices, wages and incomes policies in industrial market economies* (Geneva 1966); *The labour market and inflation* (ed. A. D. Smith, London 1968).

have to go up. This will have inflationary consequences, unless the higher-productivity industries can be forced to introduce compensatory price reductions.[54]

Gearing wages to productivity in each industry may cause unduly marked differences, set up a socially undesirable wage structure and engender wage claims in the less efficient industries.

The usual practice is to steer a middle course: the trend of average productivity is adopted as a general guideline, but provision is made for exceptions, e.g. in favour of industries afflicted by a labour shortage. In the high-productivity industries, the rise in wages will be smaller, and additional remuneration can be paid to workers elsewhere without inflationary danger.

In any event, incomes policy must not be too complicated: 'the rules of the game must be simple and strict, without many exceptions ...'[55] A criterion such as the macroeconomic trend of productivity meets this requirement.[56]

A wage rise exceeding the increase in productivity presents no problems if permitted by the country's competitive position. It is also appropriate if industry is to be obliged to organize production along more capital-intensive lines, and again if the proportion of wages in total income is considered insufficient.

In this connection, it must be pointed out that it is preferable to adopt as one's basis the overall trend of productivity since there are too many fluctuations in the short term.

Allowance must also be made for non-wage income—not because it accounts for a high proportion of the total income,[57] but because this is essential in order to secure the cooperation of the trade unions in an incomes policy.

The government must determine the rules of this policy.[58] By doing so, it smooths the path for wage negotiations. It must pay particular heed to the inflationary effects of rigid indexing of wages (see below). The government's role must not consist of occasional

54 Cf. H. Brochier, 'Réflexions sur une politique des revenus', *Revue Economique*, Mar 1966.
55 J. Pen, *Economische actualiteiten* (Utrecht 1967), p. 93.
56 *Ibid.*, pp. 93–4.
57 See the reasons advanced by P. Coulbois for not controlling profits: 'Réflexions sur la politique des revenus', *De Economist*, Dec 1965, pp. 836–46. As regards the distribution sector's income, see the section on competition policy *infra*.
58 In many cases the State unfortunately has no policy for its own personnel. Cf. *The problem of rising prices, op. cit. supra* note 3.10, p. 59. J. Pen, 'Harmonie und Konflikt in der Einkommenspolitik: die niederländischen Erfahrungen', in *Probleme der Einkommenspolitik* (ed. E. Schneider, Tübingen 1965), points out that only a strong government can pursue an incomes policy successfully.

mediation. Incomes policy forms an indispensable part of any economic planning and any price policy.[59]

The relevant directives should be complied with. In point of fact, most countries attach no, or very little, importance to incomes policy.[60]

Implementing an incomes policy gives rise to a great many difficulties owing to the lack of accuracy in the available data.[61] Certainly there is still much to be done in this field, but to refuse to cooperate at all in an incomes policy based on inadequate statistics (notably as regards productivity and non-wage income) does not seem to us to be justified. At that rate, any kind of economic and social planning would become impossible.

The trade unions are not, in fact, so enthusiastic about collaborating in an incomes policy,[62] and this is to some extent understandable: 'At its worst, an incomes policy may compromise one of the essential functions of trade-unionism.'[63]

That an incomes policy can be pursued successfully is usually demonstrated by pointing to the programme carried out by the Netherlands in the post-war years. It was based on the 'mutual confidence of the groups concerned'. Paradoxically enough, it was mainly the employers who gradually came to regard the wages policy as a 'scarcely tolerable restriction of freedom'.[64] As soon as the aforementioned confidence waned—after 1958, and particularly since 1963—the incomes policy collapsed. For this, weaker governments bore a large share of responsibility.

4. Competition policy

With so many authors—the precedent having been set by Adam Smith and Alfred Marshall—using the word 'competition' without

59 Cf. E. Depres, M. Milton, A. G. Hart, P. A. Samuelson and D. H. Wallace, *supra* note 3.30, p. 536; R. J. Ball, *Inflation and the theory of money* (London 1964), p. 307: 'If an incomes policy is not feasible the cost of full employment is likely to be secular inflation'.
60 Cf. *Ninth general report on the activities of the Community* (*1 Apr–31 Mar 1966*) (EEC, Brussels Jun 1966), p. 136.
61 Particularly in the field of non-wage income. Cf. E. Lundberg, 'General survey of some issues of wage policy', in *Wages policy under full employment* (ed. R. Turvey, London 1952), p. 15: 'The tragic fact is . . . that we have very little empirical foundation of our generalizations about the complicated interdependence of wages, productivity, level of employment, etc. . . .'
62 See in particular the unconvincing arguments for rejecting incomes policy as a weapon in the fight against inflation in *La politique des revenus* (Fédération générale du Travail de Belgique, Brussels 1966), pp. 26–7.
63 *Ibid.,* p. 9. See in the same connection, *The Economist,* 4 Feb 1967, p. 396: 'It is the job, the whole *raison d'être,* of trade union officials and of employers' organizations to haggle over wages.'
64 J. Pen, *supra* note 3.58, p. 132.

defining it and in widely differing senses, a regrettable terminological confusion has resulted.

As was stressed above (Chapter 1, C, 1), it is necessary to distinguish between competition as market structure, or pure competition —the theoretical concept—and competition as market behaviour, or active competition. That the latter is possible must be attributed to the absence of the former. In active competition, each competitor influences the plans and behaviour of the others. (He endeavours to increase his share of the market.)

Active competition is not always effective. Effective competition involves appraising the level of prices.[65] This is not always an easy matter. *Quot scriptores, tot sententiae.* Or, as E. S. Mason so rightly states: 'There are as many definitions of "effective" or "workable" competition as there are effective or working economists'.[66]

Recognized forms of effective competition[67] are competition proper, or price competition, and competition in quality. Although some authors consider that competition is intensifying in the field of quality,[68] the evidence is that rivalry between competitors is increasingly finding expression in presentation, advertising, packaging, delivery dates, terms of payment and the number of retail outlets.

In a broad sense, competition policy is taken to mean governmental measures designed either to promote or to limit active competition between firms;[69] in a narrower sense, it is designed to maintain or introduce effective competition.[70]

Competition policy—as understood in the second sense—must therefore concern itself primarily with the level of prices. It consists chiefly in combating the abuses of economic power in this field. The

---

65 Effective competition as conceived by K. Stegeman, *Wettbewerb und Harmonisierung im gemeinsamen Markt* (Cologne 1966), p. 20, corresponds more to active competition.

66 E. S. Mason, *Economic concentration and the monopoly problem* (Cambridge, Mass., 1957), p. 381.

67 Cf. the concept of 'möglicher Wettbewerb' in *Kartell und Wettbewerb in der Schweiz, 31. Veröffentlichung der Preisbildungskommission des Eidgenössischen Volkswirtschaftsdepartments* (2nd edn, Berne 1957), pp. 160, 205.

68 See, e.g., E. Bohler, 'Die Konkurrenz als Organisationsprinzip der Wirtschaft', *Schweizerische Zeitschrift für Volkswirtschaft und Statistik*, Oct 1950; W. A. Jöhr, 'Die Leistungen des Konkurrenzsystemes und seine Bedeutung für die Wirtschaft unserer Zeit', *ibid.*; L. Abbott, *Quality and competition* (New York 1955).

69 Cf. H. W. Lambers, 'Het mededingingsbeleid', in *Theorie van de economische politiek. Een systematisch overzicht met bijdragen van Nederlandse en Belgische auteurs, op. cit. supra* note 3.9, p. 330. For a still wider definition, see in particular W. Eucken, *Grundsätze der Wirtschaftspolitik* (Tübingen 1952), pp. 245–6.

70 See, on the subject of aims of competition policy, P. Hennipman, 'De taak van de mededingingspolitiek', *De Economist*, Jul–Aug 1966; E. Hoppmann, 'Das Konzept der optimalen Wettbewerbsintensität', *Jahrbücher für Nationalökonomie und Statistik*, Oct 1966, pp. 288–92.

tendency to grant excessive profit margins to distributors is one which should be counteracted.

5. Policy on international economic relations

The government can exercise an influence on supply by making it easier to import, by reducing customs tariffs or by increasing quotas. Simultaneously, restrictions can be imposed on exports.

International commitments, notably those under GATT, frequently render the use of such measures impossible, at least by the developed countries.[71]

Encouragement of immigration also contributes to the adaptation of supply to excess demand.[72]

But inflation can also be 'imported'. This is what happens when inflation in a given country induces greater demand for goods in other countries. In these countries the increase in exports will have inflationary effects. Imported—'semi-automatic'[73]—inflation may be compensated by a revaluation.[74] If the alteration in the exchange rate is a substantial one, it requires the approval of the International Monetary Fund. Autonomous action in this respect is becoming more and more difficult in the countries of the European Economic Community. Thus price relationships in agriculture are usually arrived at after long and arduous discussion and a great deal of compromise. An alteration of the exchange rate can give rise to a multitude of problems in such a case.[75]

It is being increasingly borne in on all concerned that the fight against inflation calls for coordinated action at international level. Failing this, the smaller countries in particular will experience difficulty in shutting out inflation of external origin. In the European Community more than anywhere else, a common policy on prices and wages is essential.[76] Hitherto the level of prices and wages has not been the overriding concern of the Community executives.[77]

---

71 Cf. M. A. G. van Meerhaeghe, *International economic institutions* (London 1968), Chapter 6
72 Measures aimed at increasing manpower mobility operate along the same lines.
73 F. Machlup, *International monetary systems and the free market economy* (Reprints in international finance, Princeton 1966), p. 8.
74 Cf., e.g., A. W. Philips, 'Employment, inflation and growth', *Economica*, Feb 1962; A. A. J. Smulders, 'De loondrift en zijn implicaties voor de economische politiek', *Maandschrift Economie*, Jul 1966; G. Schmölders, *Geldpolitik* (Tübingen 1962), p. 269.
75 A. Shonfield, 'Stabilization policies in the West: from demand to supply management', *The Journal of Political Economy*, Aug 1967, p. 441.
76 D. B. J. Schouten, 'Een voorstel tot Europese looncoördinatie', *Maandschrift Economie*, Aug 1964.
77 M. A. G. van Meerhaeghe, *op. cit. supra* note 3.71, pp. 362–3.

Like other international organizations,[78] the Community seems more preoccupied with problems relating to depressions than with those inherent in prosperity.

6. Direct action

Direct control of a general character is not desirable in normal conditions. Social considerations, however, dictate direct action in the fields of rents, agricultural prices and public utilities.

The fact that numerous prices are administered makes it necessary to keep a strict watch on the pattern which they follow.[79] Cases of lower costs resulting in lower prices are becoming fewer and fewer. Lower costs were not reflected in lower prices in the Netherlands in 1956 (abolition of turnover tax at the retail stage) or in 1961 (5 per cent revaluation).[80] Price increases at the producer stage, on the other hand, are passed on immediately to the retail stage.[81]

Monetary and fiscal policy will be of little use against non-flexible prices.[82]

In order to follow price movements—in this connection, it is above all necessary to 'watch the behaviour of the major oligopolies'[83] —certain countries, such as Belgium and France, compel some or all producers to notify every price increase in advance (see Chapter 5). If it thinks fit, the government may oppose the increase, freeze prices or fix maximum prices.

E. SUMMARY AND CONCLUSION

There is a misguided tendency among many economists to minimize the drawbacks of inflation and even to attribute advantages to it.

78 See, e.g., the following United Nations reports: *National and international measures for full employment, op. cit. supra* note 3.32 ; *Measures for the economic development of underdeveloped countries* (New York, May 1951).

79 E.g., E. Kefauver, with the assistance of I. Till, *In a few hands. Monopoly power in America* (Baltimore 1965), p. 207. By contrast, H. W. Briefs, *Pricing power and 'administrative inflation'. Concepts, facts and policy implications* (Washington 1962) and H. J. Depodwin and R. T. Selden, 'Business pricing and inflation', *The Quarterly Journal of Economics*, Apr 1963, are against such supervision. J. W. Markham, too, considers that administered prices do not call for any change in traditional economic policy: *Administered prices and the recent inflation* (Englewood Cliffs 1964), mimeogr.

80 W. Drechsel, 'Het Nederlandse prijsbeleid', *Maandschrift Economie*, Jun–Jul 1965, p. 489. Mr Drechsel is Director of the Prices Division of the Ministry of Economic Affairs in the Netherlands.   81 Cf. *Ibid.*, p. 468.

82 G. Bombach, 'Ursachen der Nachkriegsinflation und Probleme der Inflationsbekämpfung', in *Stabile Preise in wachsender Wirtschaft. Das Inflationsproblem, op. cit. supra* note 3.24, pp. 199–200.

83 J. Houssiaux, *Concurrence et Marché Commun* (Paris 1959), p. 167.

Inflation is by no means essential to economic growth. Full employment and price stability are compatible, but they are difficult to achieve concurrently because governments do not attach sufficient importance to combating inflation. It is mainly a question of firm will. Although all political parties proclaim that price stability must be a leading objective of economic policy—the general public is becoming increasingly aware of the problem inherent in inflation—they refrain from advocating or applying the measures required to fulfil this aim.

Stabilization policy is facilitated by identification of the cause or causes of inflation. In most cases, the chief cause is excess demand, the extent of which, however, varies from period to period and from country to country. An increase in costs accelerates the inflation process. Administered prices and competition at the distribution level also induce inflationary tendencies.

Fiscal policy and monetary policy are particularly appropriate instruments where inflation has been caused by excess demand. It is not always possible, however, to rely on the effects of monetary policy.

The fight against inflation will be unsuccessful without a vigorous incomes policy. This means, among other things, arbitration by the government in industrial disputes and presupposes a sense of responsibility in all industries and all trade unions *vis-à-vis* the national economy.

Policy aimed at introducing or maintaining effective competition entails control over administered prices, competition at the distribution level and, in general, price determination. The paucity of available information in this sphere should prompt governments to institute the indispensable industry-by-industry inquiries.

Particularly in the case of the smaller countries, the fight against inflation must be accompanied by coordinated action at international level. An alteration of the rate of exchange may serve as a shield against imported inflation but must go hand in hand with measures to combat rigid prices.

Generally speaking, direct action by the government is a *sine qua non*. Advance notification of price increases, for instance, may render valuable services.

The results of price policy are difficult to predict. The usual practice is to employ several instruments of price policy in combination.

In certain fields—cases in point being fiscal policy and incomes policy—governments nevertheless hesitate to take unpopular measures. The outcome of the next elections seems to weigh more heavily with them than price stability. Their view is that an increase in direct taxes will remain longer in the general public's memory than, for example, a moderate rise in the overall price level. Moreover, the fight against inflation demands more in the way of direct intervention than does the fight against underemployment. And in many countries such direct action is not politically feasible.

4 The purpose of competition policy.
A critical appraisal of the EEC's views

We shall first outline the views of the EEC Commission on the role of competition and the purpose of competition policy, going on to examine these views in detail and to put forward our opinion of how competition policy should be understood.

A. THE VIEWS OF THE COMMISSION

This account of the Commission's views derives mostly from statements by H. von der Groeben, the member of the Commission who was responsible for competition (together with R. Marjolin and J. Rey) until 1 July 1967.

1. The role of competition

Members of the Commission have repeatedly singled out competition as the most appropriate means of ensuring that the Community operates smoothly, the maintenance of competition being designated the essential objective of the Community's policy.

According to von der Groeben, competition 'is an essential instrument for . . . an economic system in which there is private enterprise and in which workers can choose their employment and consumers what they wish to consume'.[1] And again: 'Under conditions of competition, the price mechanism automatically ensures that each

1 H. von der Groeben, *Competition in the Common Market. Address to the European Parliament on 19 October 1961* (EEC Commission reprint), p. 6; H. von der Groeben, 'Wettbewerb im Gemeinsamen Markt', *Europa-Archiv*, 25 Nov 1961, p. 645.

country specializes in the goods it is relatively best suited to produce. . . '.[2]

W. Hallstein, the President of the Commission until 1 July 1967, is no less categorical: 'When we say that the competitive order is a central piece within the order of our Community we mean much more. We are saying that in no part, in no chapter of our Community order [is] the spirit of this order . . . stronger, more clearly expressed, than in the rules of competition.'[3]

Members of the Commission's staff have also made statements to this effect. Take the following assertion, for instance: 'It is . . . no exaggeration to state that, economically, the Rome Treaty is basically a treaty for more competition . . . It [competition] has been considered one of the principal pillars on which our building rests'.[4] Commentators on the EEC's competition policy have had their say too: 'It stands out clearly that competition is regarded as beneficial in itself'[5] and 'The resemblance between von der Groeben's philosophy and that of Erhard's social market economy is very noticeable.'[6]

It is not only for each of the EEC member countries' economies but also for the process of integration itself that competition is indispensable: 'The degree of economic integration so far attained may be said to be mainly due to the pressure which growing competition has exerted on the economic behaviour of those participating in the market. Its function as a mainspring and driving force in market integration is unmistakable.'[7] Hallstein also attributes increased prosperity in the EEC to competition: ' "demand and supply" and the market forces they reflect have been the essential elements in integration. Competition is the driving force in this dynamic process'.[8]

2 H. von der Groeben, 'Die Aufgaben der Wettbewerbspolitik im Gemeinsamen Markt und in der Atlantischen Partnerschaft', *Wirtschaft und Wettbewerb*, Dec 1964, p. 1003.
3 W. Hallstein, 'Address to the International Conference on Restraints of Competition. Frankfurt on Main, Jun 1960', in *Cartel and monopoly in modern law. II* (Karlsruhe 1961), p. 1010.
4 R. Mussard, 'The regulation of restrictive business practices under the Common Market Treaty', in *Restrictive practices, patents, trade marks and unfair competition in the Common Market* (International and Comparative Law Quarterly Supplementary Publication No. 4, 1962), p. 17, cited in D. L. McLachlan and D. Swann, 'Competition policy in the Common Market', *The Economic Journal*, Mar 1963, p. 54.
5 D. L. McLachlan and D. Swann, *supra* note 4.4, p. 79. However, H. von der Groeben and P. VerLoren van Themaat, Director General for Competition until 1 September 1967, have repeatedly stated that competition should not be regarded as an end in itself but as a means to an end.
6 *Ibid.*, p. 56, note 1.
7 H. von der Groeben, *supra* note 4.2, p. 1004.
8 W. Hallstein, 'The European Economic Community as an economic order', in *The market economy in Western European integration* (Louvain 1965), p. 23.

2. The purpose of competition policy

It is no surprise, then, to find that in von der Groeben's view competition policy 'has the twofold task of promoting integration of the markets by eliminating obstacles to competition and using competition to guide the economic process in the integrated market'.[9]

More specifically: 'Competition policy . . . calls for the establishment and observance of standards of legality, enabling workable competition to be maintained while protecting firms from unfair competition. For this is the only kind of competition that can increase productivity, well-being and freedom, on which the effectiveness of a free market economy depends.'[10]

So pride of place is granted to competition policy. Although the importance of the other aspects of economic policy is not denied, they generally come second. As Hallstein puts it: 'In addition to competition policy, there is a second, and at least equally important, field of measures which cover the whole economy, namely the various aspects of overall economic policy.'[11] H. von der Groeben is even more explicit: 'Monetary policy and economic policy, structure policy, regional policy and transport policy' are only there 'to underpin and supplement' competition policy.[12]

B. THE SIGNIFICANCE OF COMPETITION

Without wishing to deny the importance of competition, we must say that the point is exaggerated in the statements we have cited; and, in fact, this comes out clearly in the function that is allocated to competition policy.

9 H. von der Groeben, *supra* note 4.2, p. 1017.
10 H. von der Groeben, *Competition policy as part of economic policy in the Common Market. Address to the European Parliament on 16 June 1965* (EEC Commission reprint), p. 4.
11 W. Hallstein, 'Address introducing the Ninth general report on the activities of the Community', *EEC Bulletin*, Aug 1966, p. 8.
12 H. von der Groeben, 'Aufgaben des Wettbewerbs im Gemeinsamen Markt', *Europäische Gemeinschaft* (Sonderheft No. 14, Bonn 1966), p. 7.

1. The provisions on competition in the EEC Treaty

We should note first of all that competition is not given the pre-eminent position in the EEC Treaty that might be supposed from a reading of the authorities we have quoted.

In Article 3 (f) there is a negatively worded clause to the effect that one of the aims of the Community is 'the establishment of a system ensuring that competition is not distorted in the Common Market'. Then there are the celebrated Articles 85 and 86, prohibiting restrictive agreements and the abuse of dominant positions. Lastly, Article 29 stipulates that in establishing the common external tariff the Commission must take account of 'the development of competitive conditions within the Community in so far as such development leads to an improvement in the competitive capacity of firms'. Nowhere, however, is there any mention of the dogmatic superiority of competition as such.

On the contrary, we may take it 'that the signature of the EEC Treaty did not create or entail any one unequivocal conception of competition. Things are more or less in a state of flux, member states' individual constructions of Treaty provisions have considerable force, and implementing measures in this field will depend on political circumstances'.[13]

The remarks of Hallstein and von der Groeben quoted above clearly show the influence of the German neoliberalists, but even if we assume that the view expressed is 'largely a German one',[14] we cannot but suppose that the statements in question were made in the name of the Commission. The Commission's opinion certainly does not represent the views of all the member countries. In France, for instance, the coordination of individual transactors' economic plans provided by the market mechanism is felt to be too incomplete and defective, so that it should be supplemented and to some extent replaced by coordination under a national plan with stated guidelines.[15]

---

13 W. Weber, 'Wettbewerb und Wirtschaftsintegration (dargestellt am Beispiel der EWG)', in *Essays in honour of Marco Fanno, Vol. II: Investigations in economic theory and methodology* (Padua 1966), pp. 701–2.

14 D. L. McLachlan and D. Swann, *Competition policy in the European Community. The rules in theory and practice* (London 1967), p. 80.

15 J. Zijlstra, assisted by B. Goudzwaard, *Politique économique et problèmes de la concurrence dans la CEE*, EEC, Studies-Competition Series No. 2 (Brussels 1966), p. 27.

2. The definition of competition

A second point to note is that competition is nowhere defined in the Treaty. Definition is also lacking, of course, in the legislation of numerous countries[16] and in the writings of many economists, so terminological confusion is a normal phenomenon here.

According to von der Groeben, what we must strive for is 'workable competition'. This means 'competition that is effective in practice. What is needed is for access to the relevant market to remain open, for changes in supply and demand to be reflected in prices, for production and sales not to be artificially restricted, and for the freedom of action and choice of suppliers, buyers and consumers not to be compromised.'[17]

This is perhaps more a definition of active competition, in which every competitor influences the plans and conduct of other competitors and tries to increase his share of the market.

Active competition (Chapter 1, C, 1) can have good or bad consequences and only if the consequences are good would we call it workable or, better, effective competition. In other words, some importance should be attached to market performance. There is no benefit to the economy in competition that leads to higher prices (no price competition), poorer quality (no quality competition) or technical stagnation (no innovation). Where there is effective competition, which is linked to performance, prices settle down at a 'normal' level. To assess whether prices are normal, we can lay down various tests, such as the level of profits (Chapter 1). We must not be too rigid here, since large profits in themselves are not to be condemned: everything depends on how they are used.

We are convinced that it is not always an easy matter to analyse competition on the basis of market performance, and any such analysis is always open to criticism.[18] We do think, however, that performance must remain the principal test because competition as market conduct, for instance, need not necessarily be beneficial (non-performance competition) and in many cases may even turn out to be injurious.

16 R. Blum, 'Der Wettbewerb im wirtschaftspolitischen Konzept', *Zeitschrift für die gesamte Staatswissenschaft*, Jan 1965, notes that this is true of German law. See also J. van Damme, 'La mise en œuvre des articles 85 et 86 du Traité de Rome', *Cahiers de Droit Européen*, 1966, No. 3, pp. 298–9.

17 H. von der Groeben, *op. cit. supra* note 4.10, p. 19.

18 See, e.g., E. Kaufer, 'Kantzenbachs Konzept des funktionsfähigen Wettbewerbs. Ein Kommentar', *Jahrbücher für Nationalökonomie und Statistik*, Dec 1966, pp. 491–2.

We should point out here that the EEC Commission seems to hold uncomplicated views on the nature of price determination: 'Prices are formed in the market, where supply and demand determine their level.'[19] Now if any problem is a complex one, it is the problem of price determination, and the law of supply and demand certainly provides nothing approaching an adequate explanation.

The Commission, then, ignores the existence of administered prices. These are prices that are not set by the interplay of supply and demand (as they are in von der Groeben's definition of competition) but (Chapter 1, C, 3) are fixed by a single firm, by a number of firms acting in concert or by the government.

3. The drawbacks of business rivalry

A great deal has already been written about the general drawbacks of active competition—in respect of formation of income, for instance—and the government action needed to regulate it. Active competition provides no guarantee at all of optimum satisfaction of needs[20] or of maximum economic growth.[21] We would digress too far if we were to dwell on this point; let us merely stop to indicate two specific drawbacks of modern business rivalry.

The first is the increasing evidence that such rivalry results in bigger dealers' margins being allowed[22] which encourages dealers to push sales of the products on which they earn most. In the EEC this has become a typical means of gaining a foothold on the market of another member country. Rivalry of this kind—which is known as margin competition—leads to higher prices. Nevertheless, it would be in the interest of firms to use cheaper and more efficient channels of distribution. According to A. Piatier, 'It would be more effective than the unimaginative battle that is sometimes fought for more sales outlets, added luxury, further pressures on costs ... or

19 W. Hallstein, *supra* note 4.8, p. 20.
20 See, e.g., R. B. Stevens and B. S. Yamey, *The Restrictive Practices Court. The judicial process and economic policy* (London 1965), p. 111: 'There are rival theories, and no general agreement as to their applicability to different classes of situations. Thus the theory may be espoused that competition eliminates the less efficient, provides incentives to cost-reduction, and so promotes efficiency. On the other hand, the theory may be propounded that restraints on competition improve efficiency because higher profits and a sense of greater security encourage the introduction of cost-reducing methods which require heavy initial capital expenditures.'
21 Cf. P. Lambert, 'Possibilities and limits of competition', *Annals of Public and Cooperative Economy,* Apr–Sep 1965, p. 157.
22 This is a stage that generally follows that of rivalry through resale-price maintenance after 'the cumulative adoption' of the after 'by competitive manufacturers (has neutralized) its "competitive" advantages to any-one of them': B. S. Yamey, *The economics of resale price maintenance* (London 1954), p. 13.

excessive advertising: in industries where all the brands engage in an orgy of advertising, the net result is not increased sales but growing brand disloyalty.'[23]

Another drawback is excessive style changes—where minor variations are repeatedly introduced in order to give the consumer the impression that new products are being put on the market. The proportion of distribution costs in total costs rises steadily, and this sends up prices as well.

4. The benefits of combination

We may even assert that the restriction of rivalry between firms will facilitate more efficient organization and improvements in the quality of products. In fact, Article 85(3) explicitly approves, under certain circumstances, agreements which promote technical progress.

If it is true that 'the official view' in the EEC is that 'there is no proof of conflict between competition and technical progress',[24] then it is certainly a challengeable view. It may be so in certain industries—but even then much will depend on the scale of competing firms. Even if an invention or an improved production process emanates from individuals or a small business,[25] the repercussions on market performance will be revealed in large firms, because small ones generally operate in marginal conditions.

As has been rightly said with reference to the United States: 'By and large, the most competitive industries ... have been the least progressive; that is, they have developed new products, new techniques, new marketing approaches more slowly and later than much less competitive industries characterized by large firms. In addition, they have developed chronic overcapacity and, in general, have not been models for the rest of the economy.'[26]

23 A. Piatier, 'En guise d'introduction', in *Les formes modernes de la concurrence* (Paris 1964), p. 28.
24 D. L. McLachlan and D. Swann, *supra* note 4.4, p. 55.
25 W. Adams and J. B. Dirlam, 'Big steel, invention, and innovation', *The Quarterly Journal of Economics*, May 1966; J. Jewkes, D. Sawers and R. Stillerman, *The sources of invention* (London 1958).
26 A. Oxenfeldt and V. Holubnychy, *Economic systems in action. The United States, the Soviet Union, France* (3rd edn, New York 1965), pp. 56–7. The authors refer to agriculture—especially grain and cotton farming; the cotton textile industry; most industries that produce apparel; most divisions of the food processing industry; and most retailing trades.

5. Competition, integration and prices

To attribute the growth of trade within the EEC to the dismantling of tariff barriers and more intensive competition (see above) will not hold water: trade between the member countries would have expanded even if the Common Market had not been established. The process had already begun before 1958, and it is very difficult to check the actual effect of the EEC with any precision.

In general, it is scarcely possible to predict what influence integration will have on prices.[27] In the case of the EEC, however, a fall in prices was generally expected. Article 104 does prescribe price stabilization. However, it has proved impossible to bring this about. If we disregard agriculture, where there have been excessive price increases, we find that rising prices have been the rule[28] and that price cuts have occurred in few industries.[29]

It is only recently that attention has been given to these facts in EEC publications, and even then they have not been related to competition policy. In the Seventh General Report 'the effect on prices' of the Common Market is said to be 'difficult to measure . . . in the Community as a whole'.[30] The increase in margin competition is also noted, as is the consequent rise in prices. The Report also remarks upon the tendency for imported goods to be sold at the same price as domestic products even if a lower price is possible.[31] As a rule, importers with exclusive dealerships pay little attention to prices in the country of origin. Differences of 50 per cent and more are not unknown.[32] Tariff cuts are not reflected in lower prices.[33] As we have said, these facts are never related to competition policy. Since the Community's policy is not concerned with market performance, this is hardly surprising.

27 Cf. K. Poser, *Die Wirkungen internationaler Präferenzsysteme auf Preise und Handelsströme. Eine preistheoretische Analyse* (Berlin 1964); see also G. Patterson, *Discrimination in international trade. The policy issues 1945–1965* (Princeton 1966), p. 125.
28 This can be explained only in part by inflation.
29 In the household appliances industry, for instance; see *Ninth general report on the activities of the Community, op. cit. supra* note 3.60, p. 126.
30 *Seventh general report on the activities of the Community* (1 Apr 1963–31 Mar 1964) (EEC, Brussels 1964), p. 111.
31 *Ibid.*, pp. 113–14.
32 P. VerLoren van Themaat, 'De aanpassing van de concurrentievoorwaarden binnen de Europese Economische Gemeenschap', *Maandschrift Economie*, Apr 1966, p. 319.
33 W. Drechsel, *supra* note 3.80, p. 489; see also *Ninth general report on the activities of the Community, op. cit. supra* note 3.60, pp. 113–14.

C. THE PURPOSE OF COMPETITION POLICY

In this closing section we do not wish to give a detailed description of what the EEC's competition policy is (we shall confine ourselves to a brief summary) but rather to examine how it should be conceived. We do not dwell on specific aspects such as measures to combat dumping and resale-price maintenance.[34]

I. General

It was not until 13 March 1962 that the first measures in pursuance of Article 85 became operative (Regulation No. 17). The Commission was to be notified of all agreements in restraint of competition by a specified date. Of the roughly 36 000 notifications made, about 32 000 notifications relate to exclusive dealerships and about 4000 to licensing, patent and trade-mark agreements. Only about 300 agreements have been found to be really restrictive.[35] Block exemptions are gradually being issued for entire classes of agreement. A regulation issued on 14 March 1967, for instance, exempts a group of exclusive-dealing agreements from the notification requirement.

On the whole, the Commission has withheld approval from business agreements only where they are clearly restrictive. For example, the agreement between 53 Belgian, Dutch and German cement firms and the agreement between the German firm Grundig and the French firm Consten were held to conflict with Article 85(1).

Although, despite the existence of considerable price divergences intra-Community trade in some industries has not expanded at all or not to the same extent as overall intra-Community trade, the Commission has so far instituted an inquiry into one industry only —the margarine industry. This was begun in mid–1965[36] but has not yet been concluded.

No action has yet been taken against practices conflicting with Article 86, though there is no lack of cases of abuse of dominant positions.

The Community's competition policy has been mainly a

---

34 Cf. F. D. Boggis, 'The European Economic Community', in *Resale price maintenance. Studies* edited by *B. S. Yamey* (London 1966).

35 P. VerLoren van Themaat, *Economische aspecten van de kartel- en concurrentiepolitiek in de EEG* (Voordrachten van het Studiecentrum voor Bank-en Financiewezen, Booklet No. 116, 15 Jun 1966), p. 17.

36 *EEC Bulletin*, Aug 1965, p. 35.

mopping-up operation directed against restrictive agreements, abuse of market power, state aids and restraints of trade of all kinds.[37] The positive business of creating 'a constructive framework for competition' has been mostly confined to proposals:[38] the European patent, the European-incorporated company and, in general, the alignment of laws affecting the economies of the member countries.

In contrast with what we might have expected, then, there has been no neoliberal policy pursued in implementing Articles 85 and 86. Although certain basic principles have been formulated,[39] what we have really seen has been a case-by-case, legal approach.[40] Members of the Commission have shown most interest in 'the legal ordering of competition'[41] rather than in the performance aspect.

Consequently, competition policy has lost some of its importance, and B. de Gaay Fortman has quite rightly said: 'At present we have the impression that competition policy in the EEC is more widely discussed among lawyers than among economists. In view of the essentially economic-political nature of competition policy, this should not be regarded as a positive indication of its actual importance.'[42] E. Arndt gave a similar explanation in 1957 for the fact that insufficient attention was, in his view, being given to the problem of West Germany's economic constitution: '... over years of discussion, scientific arguments, sincerely pronounced dogmas and pseudo-theories put forward by a wide variety of pressure groups have been combined into a tangled maze, and the ensuing legal conflict, yielding little of any economic value, has hardly helped to extricate us'.[43]

2. Policy on monopolies

Certain principles are still influenced by the competition myth. We cannot agree, for example, with this expression of the Commission's

---

37 H. von der Groeben, *op. cit. supra* note 4.12, p. 7.

38 On 9 February 1967 the EEC Council approved two Commission proposals for directives on the alignment of turnover taxes. The tax on value added is to be introduced throughout the Community by 1 January 1970.

39 M. A. G. van Meerhaeghe, *op. cit. supra* note 3.71, pp. 354–5.

40 *Ibid.,* p. 360.

41 H. von der Groeben, *op. cit. supra* note 4.10, p. 4.

42 B. de Gaay Fortman, *Theory of competition policy. A confrontation of economic, political and legal principles* (Amsterdam 1966), pp. 296–7.

43 E. Arndt, 'Kartelle und Ordnungspolitik', in *Hamburger Jahrbuch für Wirtschafts- und Gesellschaftspolitik* 1956, p. 85.

view by von der Groeben: 'Competition among big firms, if it is workable competition: yes. But monopoly . . . no.'[44]

If combination, which is often the only means of 'gaining a competitive position in a wider market'[45] and is in fact encouraged by the Commission in order to meet competition from foreign firms, leads to a monopoly and this is economically justifiable, we fail to see why this monopoly should not be permitted. Of course, the monopoly must be supervised by the government (in respect of production and prices, for instance; see below).

The possible drawbacks of monopoly will also apply to oligopoly (which is nearly always a coordinated oligopoly for some purpose or other). It will not do simply to assert that monopoly 'removes incentives to technical progress'.[46] This may be true, but it is not certain, and the same can be said of oligopoly. Nor must we lose sight of interindustry competition. And the influence of imports must also be taken into account.

It is true that monopoly may bring about 'limitation of production', but there is a similar danger in the case of oligopoly.[47] Moreover, it is by no means certain that prices will be higher than on an oligopolistic market. We are justified in viewing monopoly with suspicion because it removes the 'automatic guarantees that the market power will not be abused',[48] but this attitude is also applicable to oligopoly.

Monopoly is, of course, the negation of competition—though it is usually the logical outcome of competition[49]—and therefore conflicts with the objectives of competition policy, but the latter must not be an end in itself and must remain subordinate to overall economic policy.

---

44 H. von der Groeben, *op. cit. supra* note 4.10, pp. 18–19; see also *The problem of industrial combination in the Common Market* (EEC, Studies—Competition Series No. 3, Brussels 1966). The ECSC takes a similar attitude, even when market performance suffers; see A. Coppé, 'Mededinging in de Gemeenschappelijke Markt', *Tijdschrift voor Economie*, 1961, No. 1, p. 36.

45 A. Piatier, *op. cit. supra* note 4.23, p. 24.

46 *The problem of industrial combination in the Common Market, op. cit. supra* note 4.44, part III, § 25; see also section B, 4 *supra*.

47 One of the tests of 'workable' competition is even said to be: '. . . if enterprises do not limit sales or production in an extreme or artificial manner . . .' (*Ibid.*, part III, § 4). Cf. H. von der Groeben's definition.

48 P. VerLoren van Themaat, *op. cit. supra* note 4.35, p. 20.

49 Cf. G. N. Halm, *Economic systems. A comparative analysis* (Rev. edn, New York 1960), pp. 69–73.

3. Competition policy and economic policy in general

Consequently, we are not in agreement with the Commission's view that competition policy is its most important task. Its competition policy can only be pursued within the general framework of economic policy.

Even if restrictive agreements are not to be used as means of bringing firms through periods of economic crisis,[50] policy on business agreements must, we think, nevertheless vary with the economic situation. Changes in the general economic situation and future prospects ought to have repercussions on competition policy. This demands a minimum of flexibility that cannot be obtained under the formalistic procedures of policy as it is today.[51]

Furthermore, the Commission should have an idea of the presumed growth of the industries concerned and of any attitudes that government may have. Some degree of planning and regulation, which is not impossible under the Treaty, may therefore be of some use.

Another reason why economic planning is essential is that the price system is ineffective as a coordinator of corporate decisions.[52] Prices have ceased to be the reliable regulators which (as suggested by current theory) ensure the proper distribution of goods and efficient production.

Planning is better left to the government—which has to make its plans known and whose actions can be controlled—than to private economic interest groups (such as holding companies) whose plans are secret and subject to no supervision at all.

'Indicative' planning only makes sense if the government has the necessary means to put its objectives into effect and is prepared to use them. Otherwise, it all remains wishful thinking.[53] All too often it is forgotten that the mere drafting of a plan is no guarantee of economic growth. Forecasting alone is a difficult enough task and should be approached with greater reservations. In our view, forecasts should certainly not go further than three or four years.[54]

On 15 April 1964 the EEC Council set up a Medium-term Economic Policy Committee. A draft programme for 1966–70 was

50 E. Arndt, *supra* note 4.43, p. 95.
51 Cf. also B. de Gaay Fortman, *op. cit. supra* note 4.42, pp. 297–8.
52 D. C. Hague, *supra* note 1.20, pp. 6–14.
53 M. A. G. van Meerhaeghe, 'La planification indicative', in *Les problèmes de la planification* (Brussels 1963), p. 52.
54 *Ibid.*, p. 51.

submitted to the Council on 29 April 1966,[55] and the Council approved it on 9 February 1967. However, the programme contains nothing but forecasts and deadlines affecting the member governments alone.[56] This reflects the German view of the matter. J. Zijlstra also believes that planning for each industry separately is a dangerous practice.[57] If needs must, he will admit that the possible or probable trend should be examined rather than the desirable one,[58] though he recognizes that for some industries (agriculture, transport, energy, construction, textiles, shipbuilding) the Commission cannot avoid considering the *desirable*[59] trend[60] and stresses the point in connection with the French plan that by indicating the desirable trend the plan becomes the instrument of training, order and progress by promoting the cohesion of the constituent programmes, encouraging initiative, counteracting waste and removing barriers to growth.[61]

Although German faith in the benefits of liberalism seems to be declining of late, it will probably be some time yet before German and French views on planning coincide. As things now stand, France is in fact being asked to abandon her form of planning.[62]

4. Competition policy and price policy

If competition policy can only be pursued as a function of overall economic policy, it will have to be elaborated in closer conjunction with price policy. Unlike other writers,[63] we believe that it should even be considered a component of price policy, one of our reasons being—as we stressed earlier—that competition policy should be mainly concerned with market performance. This is the attitude of both[64] the French and the Scandinavians.[65]

55 'Draft of the First Medium-term Economic Policy Programme', *EEC Bulletin*, Aug 1966, p. 14.

56 H. von der Groeben, *supra* note 4.2, p. 1014, states that 'The forecast will not limit the freedom of enterprises or consumers. The programme is not addressed to them but exclusively to the member states and the European institutions.' See also J. Zijlstra, *op. cit. supra* note 4.15, pp. 60–2.

57 J. Zijlstra, *op. cit. supra* note 4.15, p. 54.　　　58 *Ibid.*, p. 60.

59 Our italics.　　　60 J. Zijlstra, *op. cit. supra* note 4.15, p. 61.　　　61 *Ibid.*, p. 17.

62 P. VerLoren van Themaat, *op. cit. supra* note 4.35, p. 315, wonders how the French economy can be brought into line as quickly as possible with a Common Market based on the free-enterprise system. H. von der Groeben, *op. cit. supra* note 4.12, p. 8, emphasizes the fact that the Community's medium-term economic policy, unlike the French planned system, is oriented on the free play of the economy.

63 See, e.g., P. Hennipman, 'De taak van de mededingingspolitiek', *De Economist*, Jul–Aug 1966. P. Stocker, 'Wettbewerbspolitische Erfahrungen europäischer Staaten', *Schweizerische Zeitschrift für Volkswirtschaft und Statistik*, Sep 1965, also studies the measures affecting prices in competition policy.

64 B. de Gaay Fortman, *op. cit. supra* note 4.42, p. 276.

65 Cf. P. Stocker, *supra* note 4.63, p. 264: 'In the Scandinavian countries the law on restrictive business practices is used repeatedly to enforce price controls, which are conceived more and more as means of protecting the consumer.'

In a formal opinion rendered on 14 September 1962 the EEC's Short-term Economic Policy Committee had already indicated the connection between competition policy and price stabilization. More specifically, it recommended that a special examination should be made of methods of price determination and the system of resale-price maintenance, together with the practices current in this field, and that efforts to rationalize channels of distribution should be redoubled.[66]

The Commission has not followed up these or other similar proposals requiring direct government action, confining itself to drafting general directives to combat inflation,[67] although these practices and margin competition in particular are considered partly responsible for the persistent increase in prices.[68]

At a time when monopolies and oligopolies predominate, when administered prices are more and more in evidence, a well-considered price policy is indispensable. This does not mean that direct intervention is called for. Monopolies, oligopolies and administered prices are not to be condemned in themselves. They do, however, facilitate abuse, and administered prices are also conducive to inflation.

In consequence, it is essential that big firms' decisions, particularly decisions affecting prices, be regulated;[69] these decisions are 'no longer . . . a private affair'.[70] They are beginning to realize this even in the United States.[71] So price control is by no means incompatible with competition policy.[72]

Without wishing to deal systematically with the instruments of price policy, we must nevertheless point out one method that is often ignored of either bringing about effective competition or of

66 'Opinion by the Economic Policy Committee on rising price trends and the means of combating them', *The economic situation in the Community* (Brussels 1963), No. 2, pp. 83–5.

67 See, e.g., the recommendations of 15 April 1964 (*Journal officiel des Communautés européennes*, No. 64, 22 Apr 1964, p. 1029/64) and of 8 April 1965 (*Ibid.*, No. 65, 15 Apr 1965, p. 985/65), the second in effect repeating the first, in which measures were suggested that would keep inflation in check. One recommendation was that government expenditure should go up by no more than 5 per cent, but only the French government kept within this limit. See also the address to the European Parliament on the economic situation in the Community given by R. Marjolin, Vice-President of the Commission, on 18 January 1966, reported in *Journal Officiel des Communautés Européennes*, No. 105, 14 Jun 1966, pp. 1881–4/66.

68 *Eighth general report on the activities of the Community* (*1 Apr 1964–31 Mar 1965*) (EEC, Brussels 1965), pp. 135–7.

69 M. A. G. van Meerhaeghe, *op. cit. supra* note 3.71, p. 361.

70 H. W. Huegy, 'Price decisions and marketing policies', in *Price policies and practices. A source book of readings* (eds. D. F. Mulvihill and S. Paranka, New York 1967), p. 20.

71 See, e.g., G. C. Means, *Pricing power and the public interest. A study based on steel* (New York 1962).

72 See also B. de Gaay Fortman, *op. cit. supra* note 4.42, p. 171.

bringing pressure to bear on prices—that is to say, the furtherance of countervailing power. A powerful European trade-union federation, associations of firms who are customers of the big monopolies, not to mention nationalized industries and public services in the member countries, could by their very presence make the powerful combines see reason and could really counterbalance the economic dominance of the giant firms.[73]

Supervision of prices only makes sense if the government has sufficient power to take direct action and impose sanctions if need be. It should, for instance, have the power to enforce a ceiling on dealers' margins.

At Community level this implies that the governments of the Six should have similar powers to act jointly for such purpose. At the moment, this is not the case. The Commission has set up a working party on price legislation to investigate these problems.[74]

Coordination is all the more necessary as in most countries the government only keeps a close check on and perhaps regulates home prices but ignores export prices. (And the EEC's rules of competition only reach agreements that are effective inside the Community.)

D. CONCLUSION

We believe that the Commission attributes too great a significance, almost magical powers, to business rivalry as a force in economic life. There are no grounds for this either in the Treaty or in actual experience. While not wishing to deny that business rivalry may entail great benefits, we would insist that its drawbacks should not be ignored and that competition policy should turn mainly on market performance.

In fact, the Commission is not pursuing a liberal competition policy but has adopted a case-by-case, non-economic, legal approach that takes no account of performance.

Monopoly is generally condemned. But monopoly, no more than oligopoly, which is usually coordinated, should not be condemned *per se*. Monopoly may even result in better market performance than oligopoly.

73 A. Marchal, Foreword to J. Houssiaux, *op. cit. supra* note 3.83.
74 *First general report on the activities of the Communities in 1967* (ECSC/EEC/EAEC, Brussels 1968), § 92.

Competition policy must not therefore be considered an end in itself but must be seen in the light of general economic policy and, more specifically, of price policy. It must be regarded in fact as a component part of price policy.

5 Advance notification of price increases as an instrument of price-stabilization policy

This chapter deals with a technique which as a general rule is used very little and on which there is little discussion in the literature, namely the obligation that may be laid on some or all firms to notify the authorities beforehand of proposed price increases.

As was shown in Chapter 3, the authorities must be able to prohibit or limit increases in certain prices, e.g. by reducing profit and distribution margins and preventing any further rise in advertising costs. In many countries, however, the government does not possess the necessary powers.

Even in countries where the government does have these powers, intervention causes trouble if what is regarded as an unjustified price increase has already been applied. It is this that has prompted a handful of countries to introduce the system of advance notification of proposed price increases.

The following passage sets out to examine the place occupied by this system in price regulation in five countries. It can be judged better against this background. A survey is made of the situation in France and Belgium, where the procedure is compulsory by law, and in the United Kingdom, the Netherlands and Austria, where it is voluntarily complied with by the firms concerned. We conclude with an appraisal of this instrument of price policy.

A. STATUTORY PROVISIONS IN SOME COUNTRIES[1]

1. France

Under Ordinance 45–1483 dated 30 June 1945, the Minister of Economic Affairs and Finance, who is responsible for price policy, may fix in respect of all goods and services[2] 'prices or ceiling prices at the production stage and, if called for, at all distribution stages, by either determining the price himself, laying down a rate of increase or decrease, or fixing a profit margin or *taux de marque* (percentage which, when applied to the purchase price, gives the selling price), or by any other appropriate means' (Article 2). Actually, various techniques are employed; these are recapitulated below.

Measures relating to prices are introduced in Orders issued by the Minister of Economic Affairs and Finance or by Prefects where the Prefects have been so empowered by the Minister. The Orders are published in a special bulletin (*Bulletin officiel du service des prix*).

Ministerial Orders can only be made after a recommendation has been obtained from the National Prices Committee. This consultative body, whose chairman is the Director-General for Internal Trade and Prices, has members from the departments concerned and from organizations representing agriculture, industry and trade, small business, production workers' cooperatives, nationalized enterprises, trade unions, large families, consumer cooperatives and academic economists. The Committee's recommendation is not binding on the Minister. A Prefect too is required to obtain the opinion of a Departmental Prices Committee, which he himself chairs and which is similar in composition to the National Prices Committee, before he issues an Order.

Where Orders are infringed, a settlement may be arranged (usually payment of a stated sum)[3] provided the Public Prosecutor gives his consent and the offender agrees.

1 The author wishes to thank Mr. W. Drechsel, Director of the Prices Division of the Ministry of Economic Affairs (Netherlands), Mr. J. M. Roche, *Inspecteur des Finances*, Director of the Legislation Division (Directorate-General for the Internal Market and Prices) of the Ministry of Economic Affairs and Finance (France) and officers of the Department of Employment and Productivity and of the Ministry of Agriculture (United Kingdom) for the willingness with which they provided further data on price regulation in their countries.
2 The principal exceptions are railway fares and substitute road transport charges, which are subject to the concession system, and export prices.
3 Failing a settlement, offenders may be fined (FF 60 to FF 200 000) or imprisoned (6 days to 4 years) or both.

a. Freezing

On 12 September 1963, as part of a price-stabilization plan, the Minister froze all producer prices—including prices of agricultural commodities and food manufactures—at the level at which they had stood on 31 August 1963. This measure was followed in 1963 and 1964 by the freezing of charges for contract work for industrialists, several service (e.g. garage) charges and restaurant prices. A great many exceptions were subsequently allowed. Since March 1965, two new systems have been introduced—the 'stability contract' and the 'programme contract'; this enabled the freeze introduced in 1963 to be relaxed very considerably.

In the case of certain goods and services, other measures are in force which have frozen trade margins at various reference dates, at the various stages of distribution and importation, in terms of relative value (e.g. motor parts and accessories) or absolute value (leather and raw hides and skins).

In order to ensure that the Orders cannot be evaded by the modification of existing products or the manufacture of new ones, provisions have been introduced which lay down the method of calculating the prices of the goods or services in question.

b. Price fixing

The government fixes prices and trade margins at a given ceiling. The price thus fixed may be different from that in operation at the date of freezing. This system of intervention is aimed particularly at foodstuffs in general consumption, which are easily identifiable (e.g. milk, bread, potatoes), gas, electricity, some industrial products (e.g. compound nitrogenous fertilizers), certain fats (e.g. groundnuts), paper pulp and some services (e.g. men's haircuts, inland-waterway transport charges, taxi fares).

In some cases, only the distribution margins are fixed in absolute value (e.g. imported butter) or as a percentage of the selling or cost price (e.g. iron and steel products, furniture, radio and television receivers, preserves, chocolate, mineral waters, jam).

c. Price 'framework' (le cadre de prix)

Producers must calculate their selling prices on the basis of a number of predetermined factors which in the normal course make up a price. Opportunities for varying some of the factors are, however, limited. 'Frameworks' are fixed for each product.

The price thus arrived at—which is a maximum price—may be put into operation without the prior agreement of the authorities. The latter must, however, be able to check the producers' detailed calculations, which means that the supporting documents must be submitted to the officials responsible for checking.

Among the main items subject to this system are wallpaper, petrol, building works and the like, and pharmaceuticals.

d. 'Specification prices' (le prix sur devis)

The specification price is a variant of the system described above. Producers always determine an initial price on the basis of factors specified by the authorities. This price can be revised at any time by the application of a formula containing predetermined parameters.

This technique mainly affects heavy mechanical and electrical industry, construction and public works. It derives from the need to allow for the fact that the execution of a large number of orders involves considerable time lags. The initial price as calculated from the price 'framework' must therefore be able to be revised in the light of new circumstances (increases in wages or prices of materials), subject, however, to possible total or partial freezing of one of the parameters included in the revision formula.

e. 'Stability pledge' (l'engagement de stabilité)

Industrialists are authorized to modify certain prices on condition that certain others are reduced in order to maintain the weighted average of the entire range. Undertakings to this effect are signed by duly authorized representatives of industrial organizations. The industrialists concerned must signify their adherence to this pledge. Price scales must be sent when requested by the competent authorities. So far some thirty industries have entered into such stability pledges, which as a general rule are valid for a year but may be automatically renewed. If the industrialists in question do not fulfil their obligations, they are deemed subject to the freeze system.

f. 'Programme contract' (le contrat de programme)

This system transcends price policy and comes within overall economic policy as embodied in the Fifth Economic and Social

Development Plan. What happens is that, if the firms concerned agree to sign, for the duration of this plan, a 'programme contract' relating in particular to wages and investments, the performance of which will be examined at regular intervals with government representatives, they regain the right, to a greater or a lesser degree according to the case, to determine prices untrammelled by any restrictions. At present 'programme contracts' cover approximately 80 per cent of the industrial sector. As in the case of 'stability pledges', if the contract has been entered on a general basis by an industrial organization, each firm must accede individually to the contract in order to avail itself of its provisions.

Order No. 25626, dated 29 November 1968, institutes a procedure whereby firms which fail to pass on the tax reductions that had just been introduced or which do not fulfil their commitments are excluded from these arrangements. Firms which are excluded are either subjected to the provisions of the decree of 12 September 1963 referred to above or individual controls are imposed.

Since the events of May 1968 the authorities have tried to ensure closer cooperation between the various stages of manufacture and distribution of a product. They have been chiefly concerned to assure industrialists that their efforts to keep price increases in check will be accompanied by similar efforts on the part of distributors. A further aim is to encourage sellers to oppose unwarranted or excessive price increases upstream.

g. 'Controlled freedom' (la liberté contrôlée)
Prices are determined freely, but they must be notified to the competent authorities. The latter have a fortnight in which to lodge any objection. Upon the expiry of this period, the prices as notified may be applied, although authorization may be granted for them to be introduced earlier.

No reason need be given for the increase. If the authorities consider that the scales submitted are too high, they may ask the firms in question for explanations and meanwhile file an objection as a cautionary measure.

The system of 'controlled freedom' (which may be accompanied by price-framework arrangements) is currently in application for oil products, certain imported non-ferrous metals, assembly and cost-plus works and numerous services.

h. '*Supervised freedom*' (*la liberté surveillée*)
In this system, even the fortnight's time limit does not need to be observed. The only obligation for the groups concerned is to forward price scales to the competent authorities for information purposes. This is required for the following products in particular: special-grade lubricants, aviation fuels, aluminium, imported raw iodine, proprietary medicines advertised to the public and man-made fibres and yarn (continuous).

On 27 June 1968 (Order No. 25576) the prices of non-regulated services and trade margins were brought under these arrangements. In principle this is a transitional measure pending the implementation of the new system of 'contractual freedom' for these prices and margins introduced by the same Order.

Although Order No. 25576 does not apply to producer prices at all (whether of manufactured goods or farm commodities), even if the producers are to some extent traders also, it does cover processing activities at the end of the production chain whose products sell direct to the consumer (bakers, butchers, etc.).

Order No. 25626 specifies, in the case of industries coming under these arrangements since June, that controls on the *taux de marque* charged by business enterprises will be considerably strengthened and sanctions imposed if the documents needed for checking their margins are not kept. These firms may be required to show that they have passed on tax cuts to the consumer.

i. '*Contractual freedom*' (*la liberté conventionnelle*)
This new system is modelled on the 'programme contract' arrangements in industry. It offers dealers whose prices or margins are subject to the 'supervised freedom' system or to more stringent regulations the opportunity of escaping from these constraints. Their margins and prices can now be determined on the responsibility of firms, provided the organizations representing the trades concerned first enter into national or departmental undertakings with the 'Directorate-General for Internal Trade and Prices' or the prefects respectively. This new system is not intended to cover regulated services or margins only but to include all or most of the goods or services in a given trade.

Since 29 November 1968 the implementation of these contracts is accompanied by a system of controls—either national or departmental—for firms which have not adhered to the contracts or have subsequently been excluded (as in the case of firms which do not pass on tax reductions in their prices).

j. Complete freedom
In the case of complete freedom, the parties concerned have only to comply with the general obligations relating to all prices, such as those arising out of the provisions on publication (compulsory marking of every product held for retail sale).

2. Belgium[4]
As in France, the Minister of Economic Affairs has wide powers, which he obtains from a Decree Law likewise issued in 1945 (on 22 January).

Since 1951, the Minister has had the assistance of an advisory body, the Prices Commission. The Commission consists of representatives of the departments concerned with price policy and the most important business and other groupings (workers' organizations, industry, wholesale and retail trade, large distribution enterprises, family interests, agriculture, self-employed persons, importers, transport and credit institutions). The Chairman has always been drawn from academic circles.

We outline below the most important methods of action employed by the Minister of Economic Affairs.

a. Freezing
Whereas the last general freeze to be ordered in France dates from 1963, the corresponding Order in Belgium is of more recent date. By the Ministerial Order of 9 May 1966, all prices of goods and services were pegged at the level at which they stood on 6 May 1966. The Order was withdrawn on 2 September 1966. At the present time, prices prevailing at a certain date are in operation in respect of the following products: public gas supply, biscuits, flour, tyres and inner tubes, pudding powder, self-raising flour.

b. Price fixing
At the present time, maximum prices are in operation for rice, trade margins for meat (beef, veal, pigmeat) and Belgian and imported

4 See also Chapter 6.

butter, liquid milk, imported mineral waters, low-voltage electricity, proprietary drugs, domestic electrical appliances, bricks and taxi fares.

c. Price 'framework'

In the case of some goods (petrol, rolled zinc, insulated wires and cables, copperware, oils, certain types of cheese), producers may adjust their prices immediately to fluctuations in prices of the relevant raw materials. This must, however, be done on the basis of a scheme drawn up in consultation with the authorities. Price increases claimed by virtue of other factors, e.g. a rise in wages or profits, must follow the advance notification procedure.

d. 'Controlled freedom'

Producers and importers have to submit notifications to the Prices Division of the Ministry of Economic Affairs. The proposed date for introducing any price increase which they intend to apply on the Belgian market must be advised at least 21 days beforehand.

The notification must state, *inter alia*, the increases in cost components warranting the price increase; the Ministerial Order of 2 September 1966 stresses that these items must be expressed in figures.

In order to prevent the system of compulsory notification of price increases from arresting a downward movement, the relevant provisions were supplemented on 8 September 1961 by an article providing that producers and importers giving notice of price cuts not later than the date upon which such cuts come into operation may, if they make application at that time, be exempted from the conditions concerning the time limit or statement of reasons, in accordance with procedures to be determined by the Minister of Economic Affairs in each individual case, when submitting subsequent notification for increases.

While the Minister of Economic Affairs (unlike his French counterpart) is not obliged to consult the Prices Commission on every measure in connection with prices, and in many cases does not do so, in actual practice the opinion of the Prices Commission or its Standing Committee is invariably asked where price notifications are concerned.

3. Netherlands

Under Article 2 of the 1961 Law on Prices, the Minister of Economic Affairs may both declare a price freeze and lay down a specific price for an entire industry. Such a provision expires, unless withdrawn earlier, one year after coming into force. Unless immediate action is necessary, the sector concerned is first offered the opportunity to make its views known.

a. 'Controlled freedom'

Although there is no legal compulsion to notify price increases beforehand, the organizations concerned have agreed to enter into prior consultation with the Ministry of Economic Affairs in the case of bread, milk, margarine and solid and liquid fuels.

b. 'Supervised freedom'

At the time of writing, notification of increases in prices of any goods or services is no longer required by law but is done voluntarily. Where notification is made, reasons must be given. The underlying principle to be observed here is that as a general rule wage increases must not cause price increases; only a rise in 'external costs' may be reflected in prices (reductions in external costs must be passed on). In addition, dealers must maintain margins in absolute (not percentage) terms.

By 'external costs' are meant:

a. the price of the end product
b. the costs of basic and auxiliary materials, and the price of semi-manufactures
c. freight charges
d. advertising rates
e. charges for maintenance operations performed by others
f. official charges and fees
g. depreciation costs in respect of new investments other than those for replacing productive equipment.

If wage increases have an adverse effect on profitability, permission may be given for all or part of the increase to be passed on.

Although notification of a price increase may be made at the time at which the increase is applied, many firms enter into prior consultation of their own accord before putting the new price into operation. This is in order to prevent the increase from being cancelled.

4. United Kingdom

The powers which the government may exercise at the present time are embodied in Part II of the Prices and Incomes Act 1966, as extended by the Prices and Incomes Act 1967 and by the Prices and Incomes Act 1968. They can be employed within the framework of references to the National Board for Prices and Incomes (PIB). By means of these powers, the government can demand statutory notification of proposed increases in prices, wages and salaries and cause increases to be postponed for periods of up to twelve months. The government is further empowered to have existing prices reduced where the PIB so recommends. It has not yet made much use of its powers—there have been orders on pay and one on charges (laundries) because it considers there has been due observance of voluntary arrangements;[5] these powers expire on 31 December 1969 but may be renewed if it is expedient to do so.

The PIB was initially set up as a Royal Commission in April 1965. The Prices and Incomes Act of August 1966, however, converted it into a statutory authority, with powers to summon evidence and to call witnesses. Nevertheless, the Board's legal powers are confined to the conduct of investigations; it has no authority to enforce its judgments. It is, however, the government which decides on the subjects of such investigations. The Board has a Chairman and 12 members, with a staff of approximately 160. They are drawn from both major political parties, from both sides of industry and from independent professions such as the law and universities. The initial inquiry is carried out by a Committee of the Board, selected by the Board's Chairman. This Committee then prepares a draft report, based in particular on a steering brief of a staff working party, oral evidence from the interested parties and consultant's reports, which is submitted to the full Board, and

---

5 The present British prices and incomes policy has its origin in the Joint Statement of Intent on Productivity, Prices and Incomes signed on 16 December 1964, which laid down the lines of action to be followed by the unions, management and the government. The aims which the parties concerned pledged themselves to seek were the raising of productivity, the alignment of income growth on output, and the maintenance of a stable price level. The task of making regular overall progress reports on the policy was assigned to the National Economic Development Council, on which government, management and labour are represented. The task of investigating particular cases of price and income behaviour fell to the PIB.

amended as the latter may think fit. The final report goes to the government, after which it is duly published.

a. Freezing
Prices can be frozen, as shown above, for not more than twelve months, but only on the basis of a PIB recommendation.[6]

b. Price fixing
There is at present only one commodity, liquid milk, which is subject to price control. The scope for imposing a ceiling price was, indeed, expressly limited to liquid milk by the 1964 Emergency Laws (Re-enactments and Repeals) Act. The powers in question are vested in the Minister of Agriculture, Fisheries and Food or the Secretary of State for Scotland. In principle, they are to expire at the end of 1969 but can be extended by Order in Council for successive periods of up to five years.[7]

c. 'Controlled freedom'
The 'early warning' system for price increases and for increases in pay, reductions in hours and other major improvements is designed 'to give the Government an adequate opportunity to consider decisions concerning prices and pay before they are put into effect'.[8]

Since it is not deemed either necessary or practicable for this system to be applied to 'each of the very large number of individual price changes which are liable to occur in the course of a year',[8] it only encompasses goods and services which are of particular economic significance or consumer goods which are important elements in the cost of living. The inclusion of goods the prices of which are determined by very short-term supply and demand factors or mainly by the cost of imported materials is considered unsuitable, though the trends of prices of such goods are watched by collection of information and discussions with the industry.

The arrangements apply only to manufacturers' prices for the

---

6 See *Prices and incomes standstill. Presented to Parliament by the First Secretary of State and Secretary of State for Economic Affairs by command of Her Majesty.* Cmnd 3073 (London Jul 1966) ; *Prices and incomes standstill : period of severe restraint. Presented to Parliament by the First Secretary of State and Secretary of State for Economic Affairs by command of Her Majesty,* Cmnd 3150 (London Nov 1966).

7 *Emergency Laws (Re-enactments and Repeals) Act 1964,* section 6.

8 *Prices and incomes policy: an 'early warning' system. Presented to Parliament by the First Secretary of State and Secretary of State for Economic Affairs by command of Her Majesty,* Cmnd 2808 (London Nov 1965), p. 3.

home market, except for certain cases (e.g. where the manufacturer is also the retailer) in which they relate to wholesale or retail prices.

Every proposed increase in the price of about one hundred items[9] is notified to the government department concerned not less than four weeks before the date from which the price increase is to take effect.

The following data are usually required:[10]

a. a description of the goods or services concerned, including any changes being made in the product or in the service offered
b. the present price and the proposed price and the price trend over the previous three years
c. the annual sales value of the goods or services concerned
d. the reason for the price increase and, where this is due to cost increases, an explanation of these together with a statement of the part played in total costs by, for instance, labour, raw materials and other costs.

Discussions on detailed requirements are conducted with individual industries.

In addition, a brief assessment must be given of the justification for the proposed increase in the light of the considerations set out in the White Paper on Prices and Incomes Policy.[11] According to these considerations, price increases are only permitted:

a. if output per employee cannot be increased sufficiently to allow wages and salaries to increase at a rate consistent with the criteria for incomes without some increase in prices, and no offsetting reductions can be made in non-labour costs per unit of output or in the return sought on investment
b. if there are unavoidable increases in non-labour costs such as materials, fuel, services or marketing costs per unit of output which cannot be offset by reductions in labour or capital costs per unit of output or in the return sought on investment
c. if there are unavoidable increases in capital costs per unit of output which cannot be offset by reductions in non-capital costs per unit of output or in the return sought on investment

9 The government is in consultation with industry on the addition of further items. See *Productivity, prices and incomes policy in 1968 and 1969. Presented to Parliament by the Secretary of State for Economic Affairs by command of Her Majesty.* Cmnd 3590 (London Apr 1968), p. 6.
10 *Prices and incomes policy: an 'early warning' system, op. cit. supra* note 5.8, p. 5.
11 *Productivity, prices and incomes policy in 1968 and 1969, op. cit. supra* note 5.9, p. 5.

d. if, after every effort has been made to reduce costs, the enterprise is unable to secure the capital required to meet home and over-seas demand.

The Prices and Incomes Act 1968 empowers the government to require reductions in existing prices when this is recommended by the PIB. As before, enterprises are expected to reduce prices when this is made possible by the compensating factors set out in the four points listed above.

It is also the government's view that in principle distributors' percentage margins should not be automatically maintained when their prices are increased to take account of higher costs.

The government department concerned may make further in-quiries. In particular, it is ascertained whether the proposed price increase would be compatible with the principles enumerated above and whether there is a *prima facie* case for referring the case to the PIB.

Should the government give no indication to the contrary before the end of the four-week period, the enterprise may assume that the authorities have decided to take no action, but not necessarily that the government actually approves or backs the change. How-ever, where the official line is that the inquiry needs to be continued or the case referred to the PIB, the enterprise will be expected to postpone bringing in the price change until the further inquiry has been conducted or the Board has reported. In the normal course, the government will arrive at its decision before 28 days have elapsed. The Board will be expected to submit its report with the least possible delay and, where speed is even more of the essence than usual, the Board will be apprised of this in the reference. The authorities' aim is to prevent the total standstill period, including the time elapsing between the original notification and the formal reference to the Board, from exceeding three months.

5. Austria

Austria must not be omitted from any discussion of advance notifi-cation of price increases, in view of the part played by the *Pari-tätische Kommission für Preis- und Lohnfragen* (Joint Commission on Prices and Wages)[12] in this field.

12 W. Weber and K. Socher, 'Inflation und Inflationsbekämpfung in Österreich seit 1945', in *Stabile Preise in wachsender Wirtschaft. Das Inflationsproblem, op. cit. supra* note 3.24, p. 70; E. März, 'Zur Problematik des chronischen Preisauftriebs in Österreich'; K. Wenger, 'Die

The *Paritätische Kommission* was set up in 1957 to promote the maintenance of a stable level of prices. It consists of the Federal Chancellor, the Ministers of the Interior, Trade and Reconstruction and Social Affairs, and the Chairman and one (or more) members of the three *Wirtschaftskammer*[13] and the *Gewerkschaftsbund* (Trade Unions Federation). The three *Kammer* organizations are corporations governed by public law, while the *Gewerkschaftsbund* is a private body. Four members of the *Paritätische Kommission* represent the employees and four others the employers, in addition to which care is taken to ensure that the two major political parties in Austria each have the same influence.[14]

The *Paritätische Kommission* has no legal status. It is a *de facto* consultative body. It comprises three subcommittees—one for price questions, one for wage questions and one for economic and social questions.

The Commission's task is to exercise voluntary autonomous supervision over prices and wages and to advise the government on economic matters.

Under this system of voluntary supervision, the members of the aforementioned organizations address an application through the latter to the Commission for permission to increase prices or wages. The Commission may either reject such applications or approve them in whole or in part. Prices regulated or approved by the authorities do not come within its competence. Only the most important cases are dealt with by the plenary Commission; the others are studied in the Subcommittee on Price Questions and the Subcommittee on Wage Questions. All decisions must be taken unanimously.

Applications for price increases do not need to embrace the entire cost structure; all that need be stated is the extent to which costs have changed since the last price modification.

Sanctions may not be imposed by the *Paritätische Kommission*.

Paritätische Kommission für Preis- und Lohnfragen. Entstehung. Organisation. Praktische Arbeitsweise', *Wiener Studien zur Wirtschafts- und Sozialpolitik*, Heft 4, 1961 ; G. Neuhauser, 'Die Verbandsmässige Organisation der österreichischen Wirtschaft. Systematische Gesamtdarstellung', in *Verbände und Wirtschaftspolitik in Österreich* (ed. T. Pütz, Berlin 1966).

13 Austria's political structure has, as is known, many corporative characteristics. The *Kammer* are : the *Bundeskammer der gewerblichen Wirtschaft*, the *Landwirtschaftskammer* (represented in the *Paritätische Kommission* by the *Präsidentenkonferenz* of this *Kammer*) and the *Arbeitskammertag*.

14 For a criticism of the composition of the *Paritätische Kommission*, see G. Neuhauser, *supra* note 5.12, pp. 87–9.

However, the four major organizations (and not the *Paritätische Kommission* as such) may in certain circumstances (the price increase is not applied for or not allowed; the price is that charged by an entire industry or a firm with a dominant position on the market[15]) make a unanimous recommendation to the Minister of the Interior that the price in question should be fixed by the authorities for a period not exceeding six months.

B. APPRAISAL

From the foregoing survey it will be seen that *France* has the furthest-reaching regulations on price determination and price control. Every method of intervention is applied with a view to achieving certain aims, due account being taken of the economic and social importance of the items concerned. Price regulation is viewed not only from an overall standpoint, but in many industries as part of the process of economic planning. Whenever it is found that a reduction in customs duties has not been passed on, there is no hesitation in freezing import margins. Price 'frameworks' too serve mainly to prevent excessive profit margins.

In the advance notification system, the products concerned are considered important enough for the trend of their prices to be followed closely and for the authorities to be able to take swift action. The system operates as a transitional stage between the sector subjected in one way or another to regulation and the sector in which price determination is deemed satisfactory or at least not disadvantageous to the majority of consumers.

In *Belgium*, advance notification applies to prices of all goods and services. It may be wondered whether this is necessary: on the one hand, many price fluctuations are of little significance to the economy, and, on the other hand, administrative control is rendered impossible by the system. Even at the time when compulsory advance notification did not relate to all goods and services (before 6 September 1966), application of the system was hampered by the fact that the competent authorities did not possess sufficient staff.

Furthermore, the courts are more or less ineffective to deal with non-compliance with compulsory notification, the chief offenders

---

15 If the dominant position is not disadvantageous to consumers, no intervention is possible.

being small and medium-sized businesses. It has accordingly been suggested a number of times that the legal basis of official intervention in the field of prices should be brought up to date. For instance, it is not possible, as already pointed out, for the Minister to lay down a maximum price for the goods or services offered by a specific firm. (In France, the Minister does have such power.)

Although in the *Netherlands* there is no longer any legal obligation to submit advance notification, it may be assumed that the voluntary pledge in respect of a small number of goods is in general fulfilled. Whether the limited administrative machinery is capable of keeping close track of the price trend of *all* goods and services—the notification of price increases at the time of their application ('supervised freedom') makes this theoretically possible—is open to doubt.

In the *United Kingdom*, the authorities have certain powers in reserve, but so far they have made only limited use of them. In the field of price policy, this country is still at a 'running-in' stage. Furthermore, responsibility for price policy is spread over several ministries, though overall coordination is in the hands of the Secretary of State for Employment and Productivity. There are some significant price increases which are not submitted to the PIB for investigation. There have been occasions when the government has not accepted the Board's recommendations.

The *Austrian* Government does not possess the same powers in the field of prices as its French, Belgian and Dutch counterparts. The fact that employers were nevertheless found to be willing to subject themselves voluntarily to the advance notification procedure is mainly to be accounted for by their intention of avoiding stringent official anti-inflationary measures (notably a reduction of customs duties and similar measures for stimulating imports of competitive goods).

The results yielded by the compulsory advance notification procedure are difficult to assess, as its influence on the general level of prices is inextricably bound up with the corresponding repercussions of many other factors. At all events, it does a great deal to facilitate action by the authorities to curb increases in periods of inflation.

Effective restraining action is only possible when the authorities can negotiate with the industries concerned from a position of strength or can intervene straight away; in other words, they must be able, if necessary, to decree a price freeze or fix a maximum price, and above all they must be actuated by the will to pursue a stabilization policy.[16] The advance notification system does not in itself hold inflation. This is why the procedure has been less successful in Britain and Austria than in the other three countries.

Scepticism is also justified, therefore, as to the efficacy of the various proposals put forward in the United States, some of them in Congress, to hold public hearings concerning price increases (effected or impending) which, in the view of the President or a federal agency to be set up, would have an adverse influence on the nation's economic stability or would be applied by leading corporations in highly concentrated industries. The sole purpose of such hearings would be to 'assist in mobilizing public opinion against unjustified price increases and thereby, it is hoped, help prevent or reduce them'.[17] To put it in another way, the President would not have the power to intervene in price determination.

In order to be able to examine the merits of the proposed price increase, the authorities must be in possession of the necessary information. If only partial data are supplied (as in Austria), it is difficult to give a reasoned opinion. In the French system, the grounds do not need to be stated, since the authorities still have details of the previous frozen scales of prices for the goods concerned and are thus better able to pronounce judgment; in case of doubt, moreover, they have ways and means of obtaining additional data.[18] Flexibility must be shown when formulating an assessment.[19] High profits, for instance, are not heinous in themselves; everything depends on the purpose for which they are used (cf. Chapter 1, E, 1).

Because experience to date has been confined to 'a number of smaller countries', some authors have 'no firm opinion on the applicability of such techniques to the large industrial countries'.[20] Quite apart from the question whether France can be considered

16 In another context, similar observations have been made by C. K. Rowley, *The British Monopolies Commission* (London 1966), p. 377.
17 *Report No. 539. Amending the Employment Act of 1946 to provide for its more effective administration, and to bring to bear an informed public opinion upon price and wage increases which threaten economic stability* (86th Congress 1959–1960, Washington 12 Jun 1959), p. 7.
18 By virtue of the existence of a nationwide administration specializing in economic investigations and controls.
19 See, e.g., the set of rules laid down by A. P. Lerner for the regulatory body: 'Statement' in *Relationship of prices to economic stability and growth, op. cit. supra* note 1.50.
20 *The problem of rising prices, op. cit. supra* note 3.10, p. 71.

a small country, we do not see why this method of intervention could not be employed in the larger countries.

It is sometimes claimed that the notification system has an inflationary bias 'and thus is geared essentially to the problem of holding down price increases'.[21] It is obvious that the authorities must also ascertain whether price cuts are not called for in certain industries.

In order to prevent price reductions from not being applied (so as not to have to demonstrate subsequently the need for possible increases), the authorities must in such cases adopt an understanding attitude and grant the firms in question an 'increase credit' (as is expressly laid down in Belgian law).

To associate employers' and employees' organizations in the notification procedure (as in Belgium) appears to us desirable, having regard to the fact that combating inflation is mainly a political problem.[22] To thrust the problem entirely on their shoulders (as in Austria) is in our view misguided, since price policy is primarily a matter for the government and thus there is a danger that agreement will systematically be reached on price increases (and concomitant wage increases) at the expense of the consumers, many of whom are not necessarily represented in the bodies concerned. It is therefore desirable for all social and economic groupings to be represented. Moreover, this would give a fillip to economic democracy. The organizations represented acquire experience with regard to the price-shaping machinery. Thus in many cases they appreciate the necessity of a price increase and refrain from doing anything untoward where this measure is concerned.

In all five countries studied here, export prices are outside the scope of the notification system. Frequently, domestic prices are kept relatively low on the principle that producers ask higher prices in other countries. It is surprising that in countries resolved to form an economic union no attention has yet been paid to this problem. Without going further into the question here, we feel it must nevertheless be pointed out that similar price regulations are a necessity within the EEC if the member countries at least mean

21 R. F. Lanzillotti, 'Statement' in *Relationship of prices to economic stability and growth, op. cit. supra* note 1.50, p. 290; F. Machlup, 'Another view of cost-push and demand-pull inflation', *The Review of Economics and Statistics,* May 1960, p. 138.
22 *Policies for economic growth* (OECD, Paris Nov 1962), p. 37; *The problem of rising prices, op. cit. supra* note 3.10, pp. 12–13.

business with the curbing of inflation (see Chapter 4, C, 4). Only in the matter of transport rates (Art. 80) and dumping practices has the Community been assigned certain powers.

It would be best if all the EEC countries were to require increases in the price of major products to be notified in advance. Notifications would have to be examined at Community level too, so as to provide the opportunity for a comparison of prices and the competitive situation in the various member countries. Such a procedure would be of most use during periods of inflation.

From the foregoing we feel it may be concluded that the system of advance notification of proposed price increases, if confined to a number of essential goods, is an indispensable aid in price policy.

In periods of inflationary pressure, it can be used to exercise a restraining influence. Price supervision will have 'a psychological effect from an economic standpoint as well as a moderating, disciplinary and educative effect'.[23] Sometimes measures taken as a result of such a system are directed at the symptoms and not at the root causes of inflation, but even so they are more often than not desirable until such time as the other instruments of price policy strike home.

Whatever the circumstances, it is possible by this means to take timely action against unwarranted increases, especially in administered prices, upon which the conventional instruments make no impression.

It is therefore surprising that so many authors[24] make no mention of this anti-inflation medium.

Note at time of going to press: on 8 April 1969 all prices in the Netherlands were frozen at their 14 March 1969 level. Moreover, if prices had been raised since 1 October 1968 above the level permitted by ministerial regulation the increase above this level has to be cancelled.

23 T. Pütz, *op. cit. supra* note 3.9, p. 255.
24 See, e.g., K. K. Kurihara, *Monetary policy and public policy* (London 1951), Chapter 5; H. Haller, *Das Problem der Geldwertstabilität* (Stuttgart 1966). *Inflation* (ed. D. C. Hague, London 1962) is equally silent on the subject of advance notification.

6 The Belgian Prices Commission

Before embarking upon a discussion of the most important provisions relating to the Belgian Prices Commission, it will be as well to outline, in more detail than has been done in Chapter 5, the main statutory provisions concerning prices.

A. LEGISLATION ON PRICES

While other Ministers have a certain amount of authority in the field of prices (the Minister of Transport, for instance, has to approve prices of various services), it is usual for them to consult the Minister of Economic Affairs or to raise questions on the subject with the Ministerial Committee for Economic and Social Coordination or the Cabinet. As we shall see, responsibility for price policy is in fact borne by the Minister of Economic Affairs. In this task he is assisted by the Prices Commission.

1. Maximum price

The Decree Law of 22 January 1945[1] prohibits:

a. the sale, offering or purchase on the domestic market of products, raw materials, foodstuffs, merchandise or animals

b. the offering, acceptance or performance of any services (with the

---

1 *Moniteur Belge*, Brussels, 24 Jan 1945 (Erratum: *Moniteur Belge*, 11 Feb 1945). Amended by the Decree Laws of 7 May 1945 (*Moniteur Belge*, 17 May 1945), 14 May 1946 (*Moniteur Belge*, 16 May 1946), 18 May 1946 (*Moniteur Belge*, 19 May 1946), 7 Jun 1946 (*Moniteur Belge*, 23 Jun 1946) and 29 Jun 1946 (*Moniteur Belge*, 4 Jul 1946) and by the Act of 14 Feb 1948 (*Moniteur Belge*, 18 Feb 1948).

exception of those arising out of an employment, apprenticeship or domestic service contract)

at a price higher than the maximum price fixed by the Minister of Economic Affairs.[2] The Minister may also determine sellers' and intermediaries' profit margins.[3]

Maximum prices, or prices blocked at the level obtaining at a certain date, are currently in operation in respect of the following products:

a. Foodstuffs

1. Beef and veal, pigmeat (trade margins)[4]
2. Biscuits[5]
3. Pudding powder, self-raising flour, vanilla-flavoured sugar, corn-flower[6]
4. Flour[7]
5. Belgian and imported butter (trade margins)[8]
6. Liquid milk[9]
7. Rice[10]
8. Imported mineral waters[11]

b. Industrial products

1. Low voltage electricity[12]
2. Public gas supply[13]
3. Tyres and inner tubes[14]

2 A Ministerial Order of 25 Sep 1950 (*Moniteur Belge*, 27 Sep 1950) sets out criteria for fixing this maximum. Because of changed circumstances, this Order is no longer applicable.

3 In addition, the Ministers of Economic Affairs and Agriculture may 'prohibit, bring under regulation or control imports, production, . . . the possession, . . . use, distribution, purchase, sale, . . . transport of such products . . . and animals as they may specify'. They may even requisition such products and animals against payment. *Moniteur Belge*, 24 Jan 1945, p. 347.

4 Ministerial Order of 23 Nov 1956, *Moniteur Belge*, 24 Nov 1956; Ministerial Order of 29 Oct 1958, *Moniteur Belge*, 1 Nov 1958.

5 Ministerial Order of 10 Jan 1962, *Moniteur Belge*, 13 Jan 1962.

6 Ministerial Order of 12 Nov 1963, *Moniteur Belge*, 15 and 16 Nov 1963. (Erratum: *Moniteur Belge*, 23 Nov 1963.)

7 Ministerial Order of 28 Nov 1963, *Moniteur Belge*, 30 Nov 1963.

8 Ministerial Order of 1 Feb and 8 Feb 1965, *Moniteur Belge*, 3 and 10 Feb 1965.

9 Ministerial Order of 23 Mar 1965, *Moniteur Belge*, 26 Mar 1965.

10 Ministerial Order of 13 Mar 1967, *Moniteur Belge*, 15 Mar 1967. Modified by the Ministerial Order of 16 Aug 1967, *Moniteur Belge*, 23 Aug 1967, and the Ministerial Order of 23 Feb 1968, *Moniteur Belge*, 1 Mar 1968.

11 Ministerial Order of 18 Apr 1968, *Moniteur Belge*, 25 Apr 1968 (see also the Ministerial Order of 22 May 1968, *Moniteur Belge*, 25 May 1968). Modified by the Ministerial Order of 21 Jun 1968, *Moniteur Belge*, 2 Jul 1968.

12 Ministerial Order of 5 Nov 1955, *Moniteur Belge*, 11 Nov 1955.

13 Ministerial Order of 8 Sep 1961, *Moniteur Belge*, 16 Sep 1961.

14 Ministerial Order of 3 Apr 1962, *Moniteur Belge*, 10 Apr 1962.

4. Proprietary drugs[15]
5. Domestic electrical appliances[16]
6. Bricks[17]

c. Services
Taxi fares[18]

The Orders must be applied throughout the industry, even if aimed at only one particular firm.[19]

Certain Orders concerning maximum prices stipulate that prices must be 'ratified'. This is required when the price has to be calculated in accordance with specific directives (e.g. in the case of tyres and inner tubes).

2. Normal price

Where no maximum prices are fixed, it is prohibited to sell at above the 'normal' price.[20] Whether a price is normal or abnormal is a matter for the courts, who take into account such factors as profit, market position and operating costs.

In actual practice, the courts base their judgments on the prices generally charged,[21] thereby overlooking the fact that these are not necessarily 'normal'.

Even where a maximum price has been laid down, it is still obligatory to sell at the normal price if it is below the maximum. Moreover, no price may result in '. . . the realization of an abnormal profit through, for instance, the overvaluation of one of the price components'.[22]

15 Ministerial Order of 1 Jun 1967, *Moniteur Belge*, 9 Jun 1967. Modified by the Ministerial Order of 23 Jun 1967, *Moniteur Belge*, 28 Jun 1967.
16 Ministerial Order of 15 Jan 1964, *Moniteur Belge*, 18 Jan 1964. Modified by the Ministerial Order of 4 Jul 1967, *Moniteur Belge*, 8 Jul 1967.
17 Ministerial Order of 4 Jun 1965, *Moniteur Belge*, 10 Jun 1965. Modified by the Ministerial Order of 29 May 1967, *Moniteur Belge*, 2 Jun 1967.
18 Ministerial Order of 3 Apr 1958, *Moniteur Belge*, 5 Apr 1958. Modified by the Ministerial Order of 20 Aug 1964, *Moniteur Belge*, 28 Aug 1964, and the Ministerial Order of 27 Jul 1967, *Moniteur Belge*, 29 Jul 1967.
19 In the draft Competition Bill sponsored by Mr. Spinoy in 1962 there was provision for maximum prices for the products or services of individual firms, but this met with opposition in business quarters (cf. Y. van der Mensbrugghe, 'La politique des prix', *Bulletin de la Fédération des Industries Belges*, 20 Mar 1963) and was not subsequently incorporated in the Bill submitted to Parliament. This Bill did not in fact come up for discussion.
20 Decree Law of 22 Jan 1945, *Moniteur Belge*, 24 Jan 1945. A Royal Decree of 6 May 1935 had already laid down penalties for any person selling at higher than normal prices.
21 See, e.g., *Journal des Tribunaux*, 17 Sep 1966, p. 505: 'In a competitive economy, the normal retail selling price is the price at which products or merchandise are sold to the consumer by the majority of traders operating in similar conditions.' Cf. also *Journal des Tribunaux*, 22 Nov 1964, p. 691.
22 Art. 1 of the Ministerial Order of 14 May 1946 (*Moniteur Belge*, 16 May 1946).

3. Competition

The Royal Decree of 13 January 1935[23] relates to the protection of producers, traders and consumers 'against certain practices designed to distort normal conditions of competition'. These same terms are incorporated in the Act of 27 May 1960 to restrain abuses of economic power.[24] The regulations deriving from Articles 85 and 86 of the Treaty establishing the European Economic Community are of particular importance in this context.

4. Notification of price increases[25]

Producers and importers are required to submit notifications to the Prices Division of the Ministry of Economic Affairs, if appropriate through their trade or industrial associations, not later than 21 days[26] prior to the proposed date of introduction,[27] in respect of any price increase which they intend to apply on the Belgian market for 'all products, raw materials, commodities or merchandise and . . . all services'.[28]

Sales offices and persons who, while not undertaking any manufacturing process, sell goods (or services) and assign them a presentation, designation or brand, are also regarded as producers or importers.[29] The obligation to submit notification also applies to wholesalers in potatoes.[30]

Prior to 6 September 1966,[31] the obligation to submit advance notification related only to:

a. goods subject to resale price maintenance

23 *Moniteur Belge*, 18 Jan 1935.
24 *Moniteur Belge*, 22 Jun 1960.
25 Ministerial Order of 8 Oct 1959 (*Moniteur Belge*, 10 Oct 1959), amended by the Ministerial Orders of 18 Jan 1960 (*Moniteur Belge*, 23 Jan 1960), 8 Sep 1961 (*Moniteur Belge*, 21 Sep 1961), 15 Nov 1961 (*Moniteur Belge*, 22 Nov 1961), 10 Jan 1962 (*Moniteur Belge*, 13 Jan 1962), 9 Nov 1963 (*Moniteur Belge*, 15 and 16 Nov 1963), 28 Nov 1963 (*Moniteur Belge*, 30 Nov 1963), 15 Jan 1964 (*Moniteur Belge*, 18 Jan 1964), 1 Apr 1964 (*Moniteur Belge*, 9 Apr 1964), 10 Jul 1964 (*Moniteur Belge*, 5 Aug 1964), 22 Feb 1965 (*Moniteur Belge*, 24 Feb 1965), 4 Jun 1965 (*Moniteur Belge*, 10 Jun 1965), 2 Sep 1966 (*Moniteur Belge*, 6 Sep 1966), 13 Mar 1967 (*Moniteur Belge*, 19 Mar 1967). The Ministerial Order of 8 Oct 1959 abolishes the Ministerial Order of 20 Dec 1950, which also relates to the notification of price increases.
26 The time limit was originally three days but was first extended to ten (Ministerial Order of 7 Feb 1956, *Moniteur Belge*, 9 Feb 1956) and subsequently to twenty-one (Ministerial Order of 25 Sep 1956, *Moniteur Belge*, 1–2 Oct 1956).
27 During the closing months of 1966 (up to 31 December 1966), the Minister was empowered to postpone the introduction of a price increase beyond this 21-day period of notice (Art. 3 of the Ministerial Order of 2 Sep 1966).
28 Art. 1 of the Ministerial Order of 2 Sep 1966.
29 Ministerial Order of 22 Feb 1965, *Moniteur Belge*, 24 Feb 1965.
30 Ministerial Order of 1 Apr 1964, *Moniteur Belge*, 9 Apr 1964.
31 Between 22 December 1950 and 6 September 1966, the list was frequently extended, particularly in 1956.

b. goods or services the collective scales of charges for which were fixed jointly by or for various firms

c. a hundred-odd other products, where not as yet included in the two foregoing categories—in particular, margarine; salad oil; coffee; bread; macaroni, spaghetti and similar products; vegetable, fish and meat preserves; sugar; jam; beer; soap; paint and varnish; tyres and inner tubes; bicycles; radio and television sets; footwear; rayon fibres; blankets; mattresses; wooden and metal furniture; bricks; cement; oil products; fertilizers; rice; insurance and hair-dressing charges.

The particulars to be given include:[32]

a. the name, address and occupation or, where appropriate, the firm name, of the producer or importer

b. specification of the products or services

c. the conditions of sale (ex producer or importer or delivered domicile, with or without tax)

d. the current selling price

e. the new selling price and the date from which it is to apply

f. the increases in cost components warranting the price increase (the Ministerial Order of 2 September 1966 stresses that figures must be given).

In the case of imported products, the Prices Division requests applicants to supply, *inter alia*, the following information (on both the ruling and the proposed prices):

a. the c.i.f. or free-frontier price, in Belgian francs (if there is an increase in this price, it must also be stated whether this is in operation on the domestic market of the country of origin)

b. the import duties

c. the taxes (luxury, standard rate or turnover tax)

d. the customs clearance costs (including bank charges, health control fees, acceptance costs)

e. the importer's cost price

f. the importer's margin

g. the importer's selling price

    (1) with or without tax

    (2) delivered or ex warehouse

32 Art. 2 of the Ministerial Order of 8 Oct 1959,

h. the wholesaler's margin
i. the wholesaler's selling price
   (1) with or without tax
   (2) delivered or ex warehouse
j. the retailer's margin
k. the selling price to the consumer.

The information under *h, i, j* and *k* is only required in the case of fixed, catalogue or recommended prices. It must be stated whether the importer is the sole distributor. Considerable importance is attached to the reasons given in support of increases in distribution margins.

The provisions governing notification of price increases do not affect new products or products which have undergone radical change during processing.

Distributors may increase their prices only to the extent that the producers, importers or distributors have raised theirs by an amount permitted by the regulations. Distributors' margins, expressed as percentages, may not be changed.[33]

In order to ensure that the compulsory notification system did not dissuade businessmen from cutting prices, the Ministerial Order of 8 October 1959 was supplemented on 8 September 1961 (see Chapter 5, A, 2d).

B. THE PRICES COMMISSION

1. Terms of reference

The Prices Commission was set up on 16 February 1951.[34] Its members were appointed on 22 March 1951,[35] and the first meeting was held on 2 April 1951. The duties of the Commission are:

a. to make recommendations, as requested by the Minister of Economic Affairs, on all problems relating to the cost of living
b. to follow the trend of prices and submit suggestions on price policy to the Minister of Economic Affairs.

---

33 Art. 4 of the Ministerial Order of 2 Sep 1966.
34 Royal Decree of 16 Feb 1951 (*Moniteur Belge*, 18 Feb 1951); see also Royal Decrees of 19 Mar 1951 (*Moniteur Belge*, 22 Mar 1951), 28 Dec 1951 (*Moniteur Belge*, 1 Jan 1952), 3 Dec 1953 (*Moniteur Belge*, 1 Jan 1954), 24 Jan 1955 (*Moniteur Belge*, 31 Jan–1 Feb 1955), 27 Jan 1956 (*Moniteur Belge*, 11 Feb 1956), 4 Jan 1958 (*Moniteur Belge*, 10 Jan 1958), 6 Jun 1962 (*Moniteur Belge*, 20 Jun 1962) and 22 Apr 1967 (*Moniteur Belge*, 24 Apr 1967).
35 Ministerial Order of 22 Mar 1951 (*Moniteur Belge*, 25 Mar 1951).

The Commission is an advisory body, then, but it has the right to act on its own initiative. It should not be confused with the Index Commission, whose main function is to approve the government's monthly proposals concerning the level of the retail price index.

Within the Commission a Standing Committee has been created. This Committee is required:

a. to observe the price trend
b. to submit to the Minister all problems which it wishes to be studied by the Commission
c. to compile the necessary documentary material and prepare the ground for the Commission's activities.

2. Structure

The Commission consists of a Chairman, Vice-Chairman and members representing:

a. workers' organizations (9 members)
b. industry (4 members)
c. wholesale and retail trade (4 members)
d. large distribution enterprises (4 members)
e. family interests (4 members)
f. agriculture (3 members)
g. self-employed persons (2 members)
h. importers (1 member)
i. transport (1 member)
j. credit institutions (1 member)
k. the following government departments: Economic Affairs, Small Business, Prime Minister's Office, Agriculture, Finance, Employment and Labour, National Insurance,[36] Transport and Post Office, Public Works (1 member each).

The Minister of Economic Affairs appoints the Chairman, the Vice-Chairman[37] and the members of the Commission and their alternates, as well as determining their term of office. The Commission has an equal number of members and alternates.

[36] Since the division of the Ministry of Labour and National Insurance into two departments (Employment and Labour; National Insurance), these departments appoint the member and the alternate respectively.

[37] Prof. Y. Urbain was Chairman until 1 Feb 1964 and was succeeded on 8 Apr 1964 by Prof. M. A. G. van Meerhaeghe. The Vice-Chairmanship has been assumed successively by Mr. O. Engels (until 26 Jan 1954), Prof. A. Devreker (until 2 Dec 1960), Prof. M. A. G. van Meerhaeghe (from 21 Jun 1961 to 8 Apr 1964) and Prof. C. Walhin (since 1 Feb 1965).

The Standing Committee consists of the Chairman, the Vice-Chairman, a representative of the Ministry of Economic Affairs and members appointed by the representatives of:

a. workers' organizations (3 members)
b. industry (1 member)
c. agriculture (1 member)
d. trade (1 member)
e. family interests (1 member).

The Secretariat of the Commission and the Committee is staffed by officials of the Ministry of Economic Affairs.

The Commission's structure is such as to ensure that account is taken of all aspects of the problems with which it is called upon to deal. The Chairman may also invite 'any competent person' to attend the meetings of the Commission and give his opinion on a specific question.

3. Activities

The Commission has conducted many inquiries into prices and price policy. On some questions opinions have been divided, a case in point being the recommendation (4 April 1955) concerning resale price maintenance. It is, however, noteworthy that many of the Commission's price policy recommendations have been unanimous. On 1 October 1956, for instance, it advocated credit restrictions and rejected such measures as an export levy and a general price freeze without a dissentient vote. The same consensus marked the recommendation issued on 18 May 1966, at the Minister's request, concerning the possible reduction of indirect taxes on certain products.

The bulk of the Commission's activities, however, are centred on the application of the Orders governing advance notifications of price increases.

All such notifications are submitted to it for an opinion. As a general rule, those relating to an entire industry are dealt with by the Commission and those relating to individual cases by the Standing Committee.[38] Representatives of the industry concerned are asked to outline their standpoints before the Commission and to answer questions put by its members. Should additional information

---

38 See also 'Régime de la déclaration des hausses de prix', *Fabrimetal, Bulletin Hebdomadaire,* 12 and 19 Jun 1965.

be required, those involved are afforded the opportunity to comment at subsequent meetings.

If the inquiry appears liable to take more than the 21 days referred to above, the parties concerned are requested to postpone their price increase. In point of fact, the 21-day period only begins to run from the time when the file is complete—in other words, when the requests for information have been satisfied. The Standing Committee usually finds it less necessary to call upon experts from the firms concerned.

In a resolution dated 10 January 1958, the Prices Commission expressed its desire to be provided with the following data (for the last five years, or since the last price increase if it dates from before this period):

a. production or sales
b. manpower
c. relative importance of the parties concerned in the industry to which they belong
d. how prices are determined—e.g. by competition, restrictive agreements, catalogue price
e. trend of selling prices
f. distributors' margins, where selling prices to the consumer are fixed by the producer or the importer
g. duties and taxes
h. exports (volume and value)
i. imports of the same or similar products (volume, value, quotas, agreements and minimum prices)
j. domestic consumption (volume and value)
k. profit as percentage of capital and reserves or of sales, with any appropriate comments.

The motivation of the price increase must show the incidence of increases in costs on the consumer price. Information must also be given on any factors which have had a favourable influence on costs. The notification must also contain details of the trend of:

a. prices of basic materials and wage costs (in absolute figures and as a percentage of the selling price)
b. the wage bill and quantities of basic materials used.

The Commission's recommendations derive from inquiries conducted with the greatest possible thoroughness.[39] Whereas in wage negotiations the representatives of the trade unions usually assume as axiomatic that wage increases will send up prices in the industry concerned, the union members of the Commission regard themselves primarily as representing consumer interests: they do not necessarily come out in favour of a price increase, even when a rise in wages depends on it.

As we have said, recommendations are in many cases unanimous, which sometimes calls for concessions from all members. If it proves impossible to reach unanimity, all standpoints are incorporated in the recommendation. Although, of course, the members representing the government departments participate in the discussions, their views are not embodied in the recommendations.

The Chairman of the Commission notifies the Minister of the recommendation. The Minister, who also receives a report from his Department on the application in question, may naturally exercise his discretion as to whether he adopts it or not.

Number and nature of decisions on price-increase notifications since 1964

Period	Number of decisions	Approved by Minister	Partially approved	Rejected	Files under examination
1964 (a)	327	121	99	107	24
1965 (b)	311	131	81	99	84
1 Jan– 9 May 1966 (c)	177	69	45	63	

Sources:

a. Question parlementaire No. 20 (10 Feb 1965), *Bulletin des Questions et des Réponses du Sénat*, No. 18, 1964–5, p. 466.
b. Question parlementaire No. 19 (2 Dec 1965), *Bulletin des Questions et des Réponses du Sénat*, No. 11, 1965–6, p. 430.
c. Ministry of Economic Affairs.

If the firms concerned choose to ignore the Minister's decision, he may issue an Order freezing prices or fixing a maximum price.

39 *L'Economie belge en 1957* (Brussels 1958), p. 285.

Needless to say, the number of applications is conditioned by the economic situation. It rose steeply in 1956, for instance, after the Suez crisis. Statistics on the subject, however, are only available from 1964 onwards, since questions began to be asked in Parliament (see table above).

The same applies to action taken on notifications, data on which have only been obtainable since 1964.[40] However, analysis of such data is of less significance because no distinction is made between collective and individual cases or between important and less important cases.

In order to forestall criticism, the Minister naturally avoids systematically restraining increases in the price of items on the retail price index while allowing others free rein.

4. Appraisal

It would be an exaggeration to say that employers are enthusiastic about the compulsory notification of price increases and the concomitant activity of the Prices Commission. The business sector agrees with the Minister's being kept informed of the trend of prices but regrets that he 'is increasingly exploiting the compulsory declaration system in order to exert pressure on firms to restrict, postpone or simply waive price increases'.[41]

This overlooks the fact that the compulsory notification system is designed precisely to enable the authorities to express their views in advance. In this connection reference may be made to statements by Economic Affairs Ministers of various political persuasions. During the inaugural meeting of the Commission on 2 April 1951, Mr. A. Coppé (Social Christian) defined the Commission's task as 'preventing excessive price rises, ... ironing out peaks'. At a meeting held on 15 October 1954, Mr. J. Rey (Liberal) asked the Commission to devote the main weight of its attention to products 'the prices of which appear to be too high'. On 23 June 1961, Mr. A. Spinoy (Socialist) said: 'It is upon you [the Commission] ... and upon your Chairman that I rely for information as to the necessity of modifying or reviewing our price policy.' Dealing with the

---

40 The only information available before that date is the following, in respect of 1956: 'Some applications for price increases were granted, but in other cases the increase was either cut down, spread over a period of time or rejected.' *L'Economie belge en 1956* (Brussels 1957), p. 295.

41 R. Pulinckx, 'Le problème des prix', *Bulletin de la Fédération des Industries Belges*, 10 Mar 1966, p. V.

notification system, Mr. J. van Offelen (Liberal) pointed out at a press conference on 11 September 1966 that the persons or firms concerned were obliged 'to submit notification of proposed increases to the Ministry ... several weeks in advance *and to discuss the necessity and the extent of such increases*'.[42]

While generally speaking the larger firms comply with the legislation on compulsory notification of price increases, the attitude of smaller and medium-sized business frequently leaves something to be desired. In a recommendation dated 8 January 1962, the Central Council for the Economy expressed the opinion that the fairly severe sanctions for non-compliance with the Order of 8 October 1959[43] might serve as a warning.[44] Here, however, the ineffectuality of the courts is to be deplored.[45] Perhaps they have been assigned duties which are really more within the province of the government.[46] At any rate, it would be a good thing to update the legal basis for government intervention on prices.

The activities of the Prices Commission have called forth a certain amount of criticism, including these points.

a. Although the members are pledged to secrecy, it has been known for the Commission's recommendations to come to the ears of pressmen. When it is considered that some newspapers publish reports of secret political meetings, this cannot be said to be surprising. Even so, we feel that if fewer people had access to the Commission's files this would help to ensure that its discussions and reports are treated more confidentially. In the Standing Committee, no leaks have so far been detected.

---

42 Our italics.
43 One month to five years' imprisonment and/or a fine ranging from 100 to 1 000 000 Belgian francs. In addition, property may be seized, other fines imposed and the firm closed for up to one year. Where there is an assumption of good faith, the offender is usually requested to come into line by submitting the required notification. If, however, a price increase is notified *after* the increase has been introduced—or if an increase is introduced before the 21-day period is over—the price is blocked for six months (from the date of the notification) at the previous price level (Ministerial Order of 21 Oct 1968, *Moniteur Belge*, 24 Oct 1968).
44 *Rapport du Secrétaire sur l'activité du Conseil du 1er juillet 1961 au 30 juin 1962* (Conseil Central de l'Economie, Brussels 1962), p. 69.
45 See on this subject C. del Marmol, 'Le droit et la protection des consommateurs', *Bulletin de la Classe des Lettres et des Sciences Morales et Politiques de l'Académie Royale de Belgique*, 1965, No. 5, p. 182 : 'If the man of law is going down in the estimation of the man in the street, surely this is, partly at all events, because he is overlooking what is a very legitimate concern of our time—concern for *efficiency*, for *results*.'
46 Cf. E. Defossez, 'Mededinging en prijzen', *De Gids op Maatschappelijk Gebied*, Apr 1963, p. 346. See for a similar viewpoint: H. W. Lambers, 'Mededingingspolitiek', in *Theorie van de economische politiek. Een systematisch overzicht met bijdragen van Nederlandse en Belgische auteurs, op. cit. supra* note 3.9, p. 336.

b. The organizations represented in the Commission would like the number of the Prices Division's officials to be increased so as to provide the Commission with fuller information more rapidly. This is all the more necessary following the extension of the notification system to all goods in September 1966. Supervision over the application of the regulations also leaves something to be desired.

c. These organizations consider it wrong that increases in charges made by public services are not systematically submitted to the Commission. They rightly feel that the private and public sectors should be treated on the same footing. The authorities have no interest in setting a bad example and lowering the Commission's prestige.

d. The members wish to have prior notice of the government's standpoint on problems relating to European integration, and more particularly as to the probable repercussions of proposed decisions of the European Economic Community. This desire is understandable: in contrast with what has been repeatedly proclaimed, the Community has brought little in the way of price reductions.[47]

e. Finally, the members take exception to the fact that certain unanimous or nearly unanimous recommendations have been disregarded for political reasons. It must not be forgotten, however, that the Commission is an advisory body, whose recommendations the Minister is free to follow or not as he thinks fit. Even when they are not acted upon, they may nevertheless be assumed to have influenced the Minister's decision.[48]

Despite these objections, it may be said that notification of proposed increases and examination of them by the Prices Commission have helped to slow down the pace of the upward trend of prices: 'The fact that for years prices have increased less in Belgium than in neighbouring countries is due in some measure to the work of the Prices Commission'.[49] Because of the numerous factors which have an influence on the level of prices, the effects of the Prices

---

[47] M. A. G. van Meerhaeghe, *op. cit. supra* note 3.71, p. 361. See also Association des Grandes Entreprises de Distribution de Belgique, Brussels, *Rapport d'activité présenté à l'assemblée générale des membres le 22 avril 1965*, p. 52: 'But in not a few cases prices would appear to have levelled up.'

[48] A. Robert, 'Hausse de prix et Commission des Prix', *Nous Acheteurs* (Ligue des Familles Nombreuses et des Jeunes Foyers, Brussels 1966), No. 13, p. 3.

[49] A. Delourme, 'Quinzième anniversaire de la Commission des Prix', *Syndicats, Hebdomadaire de la Fédération Générale du Travail de Belgique*, 8 Jan 1966, p. 1.

Commission's activities cannot be accurately assessed. Its chief service has been to foster 'psychological restraint'.[50]

The system of compulsory notification allows the Minister a few days to gauge the repercussions of a given price increase on price policy. He can make use of this 'to enter into negotiations with the parties concerned and endeavour to secure, as appropriate, a reasonable compromise'.[51] As far as ever possible, the Ministers of Economic Affairs have employed negotiation in preference to direct intervention.

As a result of the Commission's initiatives, numerous suggestions have been submitted to the Minister. In some cases they have given rise to measures which have brought prices down—the price of drugs and domestic electrical appliances, for instance.

Last but not least, the Commission is a manifestation of economic democracy: it is designed to act as '. . . the link between government policy and the aspirations of consumers in general and of business circles in particular'.[52]

Consumers are in a better position to keep track of price movements and to influence the Minister's decisions. The organizations represented in the Commission acquire experience with regard to the machinery of price determination. This enables them in many cases to appreciate the necessity of a price increase and refrain from doing anything untoward. Furthermore, such experience may stand them in good stead in other advisory bodies.

50 *L'Economie belge en 1956, op. cit. supra* note 6.40, p. 295.
51 J. Limpens, *La vente en droit belge* (Brussels 1960), p. 433.
52 From Mr. A. Coppé's speech at the Commission's inaugural meeting.

Index of Authors

Index of Subjects